THE

INSANITY

OF

MADNESS

DEFINING MENTAL ILLNESS

DANIEL R. BERGER II

THE INSANITY OF MADNESS: DEFINING MENTAL ILLNESS

Library of Congress Control Number: 2017919269
Trade Paperback ISBN: 978-0-9976077-5-8

Cover Artwork by: Elieser Loewenthal
Cover Photo by: Ron Sumners
Edited by: Laurie Buck

Published by *Alethia International Publications* — Taylors, SC

www.drdanielberger.com

Printed in the United States of America.

To
My Close Friends

Having those in your life who genuinely care
about your soul and well-being is hard to find.
I am grateful to know many people
whom I can sincerely call friends.
You love me, challenge me, instruct me,
confront me, encourage me, support me,
pray for me, and sacrifice for me.
Thank you.

TABLE OF CONTENTS

BOOKS BY DANIEL BERGER II

Teaching a Child to Pay Attention: Proverbs 4:20-27 (2015)

Mental Illness: The Necessity for Faith and Authority (2016)

Mental Illness: The Reality of the Spiritual Nature (2016)

Mental Illness: The Reality of the Physical Nature (2016)

Mental Illness: The Influence of Nurture (2016)

Mental Illness: The Necessity for Dependence (2016)

The Truth about ADHD (2014) 2nd edition *(2017)*

ACKNOWLEDGMENTS

This book was made possible by many friends, family, and professionals who sacrificed time and gave effort to read early drafts and offer me valuable feedback. Specifically, I would like to thank my wife, Oriana, and my parents, Dan and Gail Berger, who both patiently encouraged me and engaged in useful discussions with me throughout the research and writing process. I wish to also thank a group of professionals for their time, insight, and suggestions: Dr. Atam Abbi, Rev. Brad Hilgeman, Dr. Jim Newheiser, Julie Ganschow, Dr. Kevin Carson, Dr. Kevin Hurt, Rev. John Hutcheson Jr., Rick Thomas, and Robert Sherman. As always, I am grateful for my editor, Laurie Buck, who deserves much credit in helping the book to arrive at its final product. Finally, I want to thank all those who, over the past many years, have allowed me to be a part of their lives in offering them Scriptural wisdom that enables them to have life more abundantly, to progress in allowing God to restore their minds, to possess genuine lasting hope, and to endure through the madness of this life.

ABBREVIATIONS

APA	American Psychiatric Association
DSM-I	*Diagnostic & Statistical Manual of Mental Disorders –I*
DSM-IV	*Diagnostic & Statistical Manual of Mental Disorders –IV*
DSM-5	*Diagnostic & Statistical Manual of Mental Disorders – 5*
ESV	*English Standard Version*
ICD	*International Classification of Diseases*
JAMA	*Journal of the American Medical Association*
NEJM	*New England Journal of Medicine*
NIH	National Institutes of Health
NIMH	National Institute of Mental Health
WHO	World Health Organization

ENDORSEMENTS

"I am grateful to Dr. Berger for his exhaustive work in delving into various secular writers, psychiatrists and researchers and distilling the essence of their insights. He has adroitly exposed the charade that is the psychiatric paradigm of mental illness in general, and in this excellent work, madness in particular. I once was proud of my insight into psychiatric illness and would routinely assess and treat patients from that mindset.

Thankfully, God through faith and revelation has freed me from that deception. He has used Dr. Berger's work to show that we may trust Jesus and not the world for the deep-seated answers for all our needs. Dr. Berger has effectively countered the secular mindset, and no matter how elaborate their information or how dominant their position may seem, they are still living in a house of cards. Our faith is established on the solid rock of the Living Word, Jesus, and He is truth. To be sane we need the mind of Christ, and apart from Him, we are all mad.

Dr. Berger has shown that mainstream psychiatry is really foundationless, built on shifting sands. The very psychiatrists who help build that house admit it. I know that my practice has positively changed by reading Dr. Berger's books – to the benefit of my patients and to the glory of God."

\- **Dr. Atam Abbi, M.D.**

"Dr. Daniel Berger is a gift to the body of Christ. The Lord has given him special insight into biblical psychology—the study of the soul (psyche) through the filter of God's Word (logos). The 'psychology' of the world is not psychology at all, but an anti-God worldview designed to create a humanistic method to solve people's problems. The most intriguing aspect of Dr. Berger's book is that he uses humanistic theorists' words to affirm their fallacies. But he does not stop with using their thoughts to debunk their false theories; he gives you a theological framework derived from God's Word that provides practical answers to the reality of madness. If you want to have a clearer understanding of mental illness, let this book, *The Insanity of Madness*, be your starting point. You'll love it!"

- **Rick Thomas, author, speaker, instructor, counselor**

"The modern day mental health system has become one of the greatest tools of the deceiver to lead many souls away from the infallible, inerrant, and unchanging truths of the Gospel. Dr. Berger humbly presents the truth to those who have rejected or have attempted to redefine the truth of God's Word. I believe the pages of this book will leave the unbeliever and the skeptic without excuse and will reveal why the psychiatric system continues to fail. Wisdom cries out from each page and points the reader back to God's Word, the only source of truth and hope for those who are blinded by the god of this age. I pray that many souls will come to their senses and be released from one of the greatest deceptions of our day."

- **Pastor Jeff Colón, MDiv, President of Lighthouse Biblical Counseling Center, IABC Exec. Board Member**

CHAPTER 1

INTRODUCTION

"There is no definition of a mental disorder . . . I mean you can't define it."[1]
Allen Frances, Chair of the *DSM-IV* Task Force and Former Head of Psychiatry at Duke University Medical School

"To define [mental] illness and [mental] health is an almost impossible task."[2]
Karl Menninger, psychiatrist

What is mental illness? Can it be objectively and precisely defined? It is clear that the concept—historically called madness[3]—increasingly shapes not only societal structure but also our views of anthropology; furthermore, it greatly impacts everyday life as well as the law and order of our society. But is mental illness a precise concept or a fluid social construct?

---

[1] Quoted by Gary Greenberg, *The Book of Woe: The DSM and the Unmaking of Psychiatry* (New York: Blue Rider Press, 2013), 23.

[2] Karl Menninger, *The Vital Balance: The Life Process in Mental Health and Illness* (New York: Viking Press, 1968), 77.

[3] In the nineteenth century, psychiatrists replaced the word *madness* with the term *mental illness* (Petteri Pietikäinen, *Madness: A History* [New York: Routledge, 2015], 3). These words will be considered together unless otherwise noted.

In ancient Roman law, the concept of madness was well-defined and divided into two categories: the "insane" and the "idiots." Psychiatrist Isaac Ray, who published the first American textbook of forensic psychiatry,[4] wrote in 1838 that "in the [ancient] Roman law the insane or *dementes*, are divided into two classes; those whose understanding is weak or null, *mente capti* [lit. mind taken or demented], and those who are restless and furious, *furiosi* [mad or manic[5]]."[6] *Madness* was the term widely accepted to describe "manic restlessness, wildness and loss of self-control."[7]

At the same time Dr. Ray published his psychiatric textbook, the U.S. government utilized the terms *insane* and *idiotic* to distinguish between those who were mad and those who had physical ailments that hindered or impaired intelligence, sensory processing, and social and motor skills (e.g., autism and Alzheimer's disease). Psychiatrist Jeffrey Lieberman remarks on this history,

> The 1840 Census added a new disability—mental illness—which was tabulated by means of a single checkbox labeled "insane and idiotic." All the myriad mental and developmental disorders were lumped together within this broad category, and no instructions were provided to the U.S. Marshals tasked with collecting census data for determining whether a citizen should have her "insane and idiotic" box checked off.[8]

Lieberman offers further clarity in showing how the term *insanity* was used to describe

---

[4] Group for the Advancement of Psychiatry, "The History of Psychiatry 19th Century," YouTube video, 31.45, October 5, 2017, https://m.youtube.com/watch?feature=youtu.be&v=TFoJ0b4v3hY: 18:45-55.

[5] *Frenzy* and *mania* were used interchangeably: "Mania denoted chaotic thoughts, frenzy, anger and delirium without fever" (Pietikäinen, *Madness*, 18).

[6] Isaac Ray, *A Treatise on the Medical Jurisprudence of Insanity* (Boston: Charles C. Little and James Brown, 1838) 4.

[7] Pietikäinen, *Madness*, 7.

[8] Jeffrey A. Lieberman, *Shrinks: the Untold Story of Psychiatry* (New York: Little, Brown and Company, 2015), 89.

> any mental disturbance severe enough to warrant institutionalization, encompassing what we would now consider schizophrenia, bipolar disorder, [and] depression . . .[9]

These types of psychiatric constructs have in the last two centuries come to represent madness or serious mental illnesses. Lieberman also notes that

> "Idiocy" likely referred to any reduced level of intellectual function, which today we would subdivide into Down syndrome, autism, Fragile X Syndrome, cretinism, and other conditions.[10]

Though insanity and idiocy were both once considered disabilities, they were no-less understood to be distinct problems.

But these concepts are also different in how they are defined. In contrast to the idea of idiocy or intellectual disability, which is widely accepted as a fixed definition and not typically questioned, a precise definition of madness has seemingly eluded prominent theorists and clinicians for the last two centuries. Dr. Ray explained this trend in the early 1800s:

> What is the precise meaning of this term [insanity/madness]? It is not easy to gather from the observations of various high legal authorities who have attempted to fix its meaning. It seems to be agreed, that it is not idiocy, nor lunacy, nor imbecility, but beyond this all unanimity is at an end.[11]

Are there still people or organizations "attempting to fix its meaning?" Can madness be objectively defined apart from any collusion, or does it remain an imprecise concept?

Though the ancient Romans were clear on defining madness, French psychiatrists during the French Revolution (1789-99) made terms imprecise and the definition of madness became muddled. Dr. Ray references this occurrence: "The French and Prussian codes make use of the terms *démence*, *fureur* and

---

[9] Ibid.

[10] Ibid., 89.

[11] Ray, *Medical Jurisprudence of Insanity*, 6.

imbécillite without pretending to define them."[12] This imprecision in defining madness was the result of the philosophical belief that dominated the French Revolution and which suggested that truth was not absolute. With the popularity of French psychiatrist Philippe Pinel—considered by many historians as one of the principal founders of psychiatry[13]— and the acceptance and promotion of his genetic theory of madness throughout the world,[14] the French belief that madness (as with truth) was abstract and could not be objectively defined would eventually come to represent a common perspective worldwide.

Like French psychiatrists during the Revolution, many of today's prominent American psychiatrists and humanistic psychologists insist not only that an objective definition of madness/mental illness is non-existent, but also that it can never be precisely determined. Take, for example, the comments made by Allen Frances, the chair of the *Diagnostic and Statistical Manual-IV* task force, former head of Duke University's school of psychiatry, and considered at the turn of the twenty-first century to be "perhaps the most powerful psychiatrist in America"[15]:

> I have reviewed dozens of definitions of mental disorder (and have written one myself in *DSM-IV*) and find none of them the slightest bit helpful either in determining which conditions should be considered mental disorders or not, or in deciding who is sick and who is not.[16]

In a similar fashion, psychiatrist and historian of madness Petteri Pietikäinen suggests that "there is ambiguity regarding the definition of madness. . . . There have not been, and there will

---

[12] Ibid., 4.

[13] Allen Frances, *Saving Normal: An Insider's Revolt against Diagnosis, DSM-5, Big Pharma, and the Medicalization of Ordinary Life* (New York: HarperCollins, 2013), 56.

[14] Edward Shorter, *A History of Psychiatry: From the Era of the Asylum to the Age of the Prozac* (New York: John Wiley & Sons, 1997), 29.

[15] Greenberg, *Book of Woe,* 22.

[16] Frances, *Saving Normal*, 17.

never be, universal and timeless rules regarding how madness manifests itself."[17] Clearly, great confusion and often heated disagreement exists among prominent psychiatrists, psychologists, and sociologists over what constitutes mental illness.

An example of this contention is the battle which occurred behind the scenes during the formation of the *Diagnostic and Statistical Manual of Mental Disorders,* 5th edition, (hereafter referred to as the *DSM-5)* – the book regarded by many within the mental health field to be the premier yet imprecise definition and classification of mental illness. Jeffrey Lieberman, former president-elect of the American Psychiatric Association (hereafter referred to as APA) and overseer of the publication of the *DSM-5,* explains,

> A firestorm erupted. *At issue was the question of how to define mental illnesses in the digital age* [emphasis added]. Not only did far more empirical data and clinical knowledge exist than ever before, but there were myriad powerful stakeholders – including commercial, governmental, medical, and educational institutions, as well as patient advocacy groups – who would be significantly affected by any changes in the *DSM*. Would the public's interest be served by allowing experts to work on revisions behind a protective veil? Or was it better to allow the debates over diagnoses (which would inevitably be heated and contentious) to play out before the public eye?[18]

Journalist Gary Greenberg remarks on the APA's dispute over defining mental illness,

> This is hardly the first time that defining mental illness has led to rancor within the profession. It happened in 1993, when feminists denounced Frances for considering the inclusion of "late luteal phase dysphoric disorder" (formerly known as premenstrual syndrome) as a possible diagnosis for *DSM-IV*. It happened in 1980, when psychoanalysts objected to the removal of the word neurosis – their bread and butter – from the *DSM-III*. It happened in 1973, when gay psychiatrists, after years of loud protest, finally forced a reluctant APA to acknowledge that homosexuality was not and never had been an illness. Indeed, it's been happening since at least 1922, when two prominent psychiatrists warned that a planned change to the

---

[17] Pietikäinen, *Madness*, 3.

[18] Lieberman, *Shrinks*, 277.

> nomenclature would be tantamount to declaring that "the whole world is, or has been, insane."[19]

Since the French Revolution, defining mental illness has not just been difficult; it has been contentious and controversial.

In the end, the *DSM-5*—created, owned, and published by the APA—further opened the door for madness to be understood as a muddled and imprecise idea—one that is seemingly difficult to define. Under its main heading "Definition of a Mental Disorder," the *DSM-5* itself states that "no definition can capture all aspects of all disorders in the range contained in the *DSM-5*."[20] Elsewhere, the APA insists in the *DSM-5* that

> the symptoms contained in the respective *diagnostic criteria sets do not constitute comprehensive definitions* of underlying disorders, which encompass cognitive, emotional, behavioral, and physiological processes that are far more complex than can be described in these brief summaries. *Rather, they are intended to summarize characteristic syndromes of signs and symptoms that point to an underlying disorder* with a characteristic developmental history, biological and environmental risk factors, neuropsychological and physiological correlates, and typical clinical course. [emphases added][21]

The APA even acknowledges that its imprecise definition of mental illness is not intended for everyone's use. For example, the APA cautions its application in forensic and legal situations:

> It is important to note that the definition of mental disorder included in *DSM-5* was developed to meet the needs of clinicians, public health professionals, and research investigators rather than all of the technical needs of the courts and legal professionals.[22]

According to the APA as presented in the *DSM-5*, no precise definition exists that can fully explain the modern concept of

---

[19] Gary Greenberg, "Inside the Battle to Define Mental Illness," *Wired Magazine Online*, December 27, 2010, https://www.wired.com/2010/12/ff_dsmv/.

[20] American Psychiatric Association, *Diagnostic and Statistical Manual of Mental Disorders*, 5th ed. (Washington, DC: American Psychiatric Publishing, 2013), 20. Hereafter referred to as the *DSM-5*.

[21] Ibid., 19.

[22] Ibid., 25.

mental illness or even individual constructs of what was once called madness. Elsewhere, the APA admits that its imprecise "definition of mental disorder was developed for clinical, public health, and research purposes."[23] The *DSM*, then, does not give an objective definition of madness; rather it is a categorization of behavior, which many clinicians claim indicates invisible diseases of the mind.

If those who allegedly possess the most knowledge about madness cannot themselves objectively define it, then what does that say of society at large, which is burdened and struggling with that imprecision? Undoubtedly, psychiatrists and other clinicians realize the pressing need to define and figure out the seeming mystery that is known as madness. Many sociologists too hope that scientific research will soon "begin to solve the great human mystery of mental abnormality. Mental illness is arguably the last large class of human affliction to be demystified."[24] What makes madness or mental illness mysterious, though, is not the lack of objective evidence, but the abundance of spurious claims and unproved beliefs about madness that have been accepted without any empirical evidence. Professor of Psychiatry at Boston University School of Medicine, Bessel van der Kolk observes that

> Psychiatry, as a subspecialty of medicine, aspires to define mental illness as precisely as, let's say, cancer of the pancreas, or streptococcal infection of the lungs. However, given the complexity of mind, brain, and human attachment systems, *we have not come even close to achieving that sort of precision. Understanding what is "wrong" with people currently is more a question of the mind-set of the practitioner* (and what insurance companies will pay for) *than of verifiable, objective facts* [emphases added].[25]

---

[23] Ibid., 20.

[24] Ethan Watters and Richard Ofshe, *Therapy's Delusions: The Myth of the Unconscious and The Exploitation of Today's Walking Worried* (New York: Simon and Schuster, 1999), 240.

[25] Bessel van der Kolk, *The Body Keeps the Score: Brain, Mind, and Body in the Healing of Trauma* (New York: Penguin, 2014), 137.

How ironic that defining alleged abnormal or impairing mindsets is difficult because people have different subjective beliefs about how thoughts and behavior should be interpreted, explained, and approached!

Defining mental illness has clearly shown to be a difficult task for most. Does the difficulty exist because, as Dr. Van der Kolk indicates, the idea of madness is a matter of one's faith? Or is a definition difficult to create because people are genuinely not sure what being insane or mentally ill actually is? Is defining mental illness difficult because it represents something opposed to our own individual and collective belief systems, or have we unwittingly agreed upon a definition of mental illness and simply ignored, overlooked, or even denied its true substance? Maybe just as important is the question: Why do we judge people to be mad when the idea merely reflects something we are not sure of, is developed for our own personal use, or exposes our own subjective beliefs? To be labeled as mentally ill is a serious and life-altering event; should we not then take more care in the accuracy of the labels (and their consequences) that we impose on others?

To answer these questions, we will need to seek out answers to other foundational questions about madness, which include: What are clear objective aspects or elements of historical madness and today's concept of mental illness? What were common objective means to recognize, identify, or diagnose madness seen throughout history? Is there only one type of madness with varying manifestations, or are there different types of mental illness? Is the concept of insanity different across various cultures throughout history or are we referring to one foundational idea when we speak of mental illness? These questions have perplexed leading theorists and practitioners, but until they are answered, a precise definition and an understanding of what it means to be mad will continue to elude humanity.

It is safe to assume that though most readers have a preconception of mental illness based upon their worldview, many may be unaware of the fluidity and subjectivity surrounding the concept of madness. The construct's imprecision and lack of clear definition are also why significant questions are left unanswered and remedies for madness continue to elude counselors, physicians, and researchers. If we cannot objectively, reliably, and clearly define madness, then there can be no beneficial dialogue or debate. If we, however, can arrive at a clear and objective definition, then we have a valid starting point to genuinely help those who meet the criteria.

In fact, resolving every human problem (whether medical, spiritual, financial, social etc.) begins by precisely determining the underlying problem. From this starting point, a cause can be pursued, and thereafter, a solution can be discovered. Without clear understanding and an objective definition, however, finding a valid pathology/etiology[26] and a reliable solution for mental illness will continue to be an exercise in futility.

Many leading theorists and researchers, though, insist that by searching endlessly for causes according to their theories, both a definition and remedy will eventually be discovered. The absence of an objective definition of madness perhaps explains why few, if any, are being cured from insanity within the current mental health system.

Furthermore, if madness is not an objective reality or we continue to maintain the notion that mental illness cannot be objectively defined, then continuing to insist on the existence of mental illness may very well be insanity itself. Yet, it is clear that many in society are burdened with undeniable and similar mental anguish and behavioral problems. So, surely there must exist an objective definition.

There are only two possible conclusions to this study: (1) if madness can be precisely defined, then its cause and solution can be pursued with clear purpose, and many of the mysteries

---

[26] *Pathology* is the science of causes and effects of diseases, whereas *etiology* is the investigation of what causes something.

surrounding the idea can be solved. (2) On the other hand, if madness can never be defined, then mental illness will remain theoretical, powerless to help individuals and society, while still reshaping social and anthropological beliefs without empirical support.

The fluidity and vagueness of madness exists—in large part—because truth has been ignored or rejected in favor of maintaining speculative theories. Without both a standard of normalcy and a willingness to accept empirical truth, madness will continue to be a nonspecific and sweeping idea.[27] But what if differing philosophies—"mindsets" as Dr. Van der Kolk calls them[28]—are set aside and objective facts and consistent aspects of lunacy are considered? Then, an objective definition of mental illness can emerge. Establishing a clear and precise definition of mental illness will require the reader to consider the history of madness and to recognize common threads and theories, definitions, and practices that are alike across various times, cultures, and even antithetical worldviews.

The same prominent mental health figures who assert that madness cannot be objectively defined also insist that utilitarianism represents the only means to arrive at both a definition of normalcy and a definition of mental illness.[29] It is true that consensus is not always an indication of truth; however, if an idea has been agreed upon throughout centuries and across cultures and it has clear empirical supporting evidence, then we would do well to deeply consider how we can justly regard that idea. What may not be clear to the reader up to this point are the specific aspects of madness that are consistently agreed upon and have been throughout history. Too

---

[27] Daniel R. Berger II, *Mental Illness: The Necessity for Faith and Authority* (Taylors, SC: Alethia International Publications, 2016), 30-44.

[28] Van der Kolk, *Body Keeps the Score*, 137.

[29] Frances, *Saving Normal*, 5.

often, these elements have been overlooked in forming a true and precise definition of madness.

To some degree, the psychiatric claim of utilitarianism — that the majority need to agree in order to arrive at truth — will not only be discussed but allowed to be considered. If agreement is realized across history concerning what constitutes madness, then such uniformity makes truth clearer. Again, I stress that utilitarianism does not make something true or false; if the entire world doubted that gravity exists, the existence of gravity would remain unchanged: "It is the nature, after all, of commonly shared delusions that they do not appear delusional during the time they are commonly held."[30] But when empirical evidence, prominent religions, philosophers, psychiatrists, and atheists all agree, then it would be imprudent — one might even say insane — not to at least consider the available facts. As this book will expose, there does exist a singular idea of madness that spans across the history of humanity and objectively establishes what today's mental health professionals and social theorists have been unable to do or have avoided doing: precisely define mental illness.

If madness cannot be objectively defined, what exactly are we concerned about regarding how people think and behave? There must be some observable, objective, and reliable standard of measurement, or madness becomes a speculative, completely unscientific, and even illogical idea. Instead of theorizing about mental illness and creating constructs to imprecisely describe and classify observable behavior that insanity produces, we must know with precision what it is that we are diagnosing and attempting to remedy.

Let us be fair and bring further clarity to this discussion as it begins. Because the modern concept of madness — as pointed out — is a fluid and imprecise construct that can be subjectively defined according to one's beliefs, many will disregard the possibility of objectively defining madness before even

---

[30] Watters and Ofshe, *Therapy's Delusions*, 241.

considering the evidence in this book. Some already may believe that madness cannot be defined; such a belief is still a definition though. Still others are curious—cautiously or eagerly approaching the notion that madness can be understood.

One thing that all readers can agree upon is that truth must form the definition of mental illness. Therefore, an objective definition will be achieved in this book based entirely on consistent truth revealed throughout history. If the reader will objectively consider historical accounts of madness—carefully observing shared elements from differing theories and clear patterns across all cultures and throughout history, then an objective definition of madness will emerge.

What will also come to light from this study of insanity is a clear definition of normalcy (anthropology). Normalcy and madness cannot be disconnected: either madness is viewed as a deviance from normal or it is understood as part of human nature. Psychiatrist Jurgen Ruesch and anthropologist Gregory Bateson explained in the early 1950s that psychiatrists desired, and still do today, to arrive at a definition or standard of normalcy by first discovering and defining madness:

> Since the psychiatrist's attention is focused on deviation, and since he has little or no training in normal psychology, he tends to construct a hypothetical norm by averaging the exact opposites of those features he sees in his patients.[31]

By asserting what they believe to be abnormal human mindsets and behaviors, psychiatrists have formed their own view of normalcy.

But what if after discovering what madness is objectively, we also come to realize that we are all at least a bit mad, and therefore, madness should not be viewed as an abnormality? What if one aspect of normalcy permits us to recognize only how madness manifests itself in those that differ from ourselves? What if only the madness that makes us personally or

---

[31] Jurgen Ruesch and Gregory Bateson, *Communication: Social Matrix of Psychiatry* (New York: Norton, 1951), 71.

corporately uncomfortable and causes society as a whole to be disturbed or threatened is being recognized as madness? What if madness—by an objective definition—encompasses more than what we find repulsive, disturbing, or confounding and instead explains human nature? Harvard University published a study in 2006, which revealed a startling conclusion about the state of mind of the American population:

> A recent survey estimated that nearly half of all Americans will suffer a mental illness during their lifetimes. Harvard Medical School professor of health policy Ronald Kessler headed the two-year study, which polled 9,000 adults across the country, varying in age, education level, and marital status. Researchers conducted home-based, face-to-face interviews, using the World Health Organization's (WHO) diagnostic mental-health survey. They found that 29 percent of people experience some form of anxiety disorder, closely followed by impulse-control disorders (25 percent) and mood disorders (20 percent). Most cases begin in adolescence or early adulthood, and often, more than one disorder will strike simultaneously. The study has sparked heated controversy. Critics argue that the numbers reflect a gross inflation of the meaning of "disease" that blurs the line between "real" disorders and normal forms of emotional and mental suffering.[32]

The lines are blurred between who is mentally ill and who is healthy because what is normal and abnormal have not been objectively defined. Whether everyone is mad, half of us are, very few of us are, or none of us are, objectively defining mental illness will eliminate ambiguity and resolve such confusion. All of these aforementioned questions deserve attention and will be examined in this book.

Finally, it is possible that in seeking to objectively define mental illness, we will discover that one of our greatest forms of insanity is to continue claiming madness exists while denying its true nature. As crazy as that may sound, we will discover that it is truly insane to continue believing that mental illness exists and that people have it without being able to objectively define it.

---

[32] Ashley Pettus, "Psychiatry by Prescription: Do Psychotropic Drugs Blur the Boundaries between Illness and Health?" *Harvard Magazine Online*, July-August 2006, http://harvardmagazine.com/2006/07/psychiatry-by-prescripti.html.

CHAPTER 2

DEFINING MADNESS

"In a tectonic battle for the very soul of psychiatry, a battle waged over the definition of mental illness."[33]
Jeffrey Lieberman, former president-elect of the APA

"Madness seems to be a relative matter. Paranoia is in the eye of the beholder."[34]
Lawrie Reznek, Professor of Psychiatry at the University of Toronto

Well before physicians transformed the idea of madness into a disease concept, it was clearly defined and recognizable. As the historian of psychiatry and insanity Edward Shorter acknowledges, "Human society has always known psychiatric illness [madness], and has always had ways of coping with it."[35] In fact, the *Group for the Advancement of Psychiatry* recognizes that though terms and surrounding theories of madness/mental illness have changed, the core elements, diagnostic tools, and the necessity of rituals to restore the mind have remained the same:

> The active ingredients of mental health diagnosis and treatment seem to apply in all cultures. They include identification of behaviors or mood states regarded as out of balance (with self, family, culture, general health, shared values, or spiritual domains), the presence of a

---

[33] Lieberman, *Shrinks*, 88.

[34] Lawrie Reznek, *Delusions and Madness of the Masses* (New York: Rowman and Littlefield, 2010), 26.

[35] Shorter, *A History of Psychiatry*, 1.

> leader (shaman, priest, or identified medicine-person), and a set of rituals known within the culture to restore balance (somatic interventions, trance states, sleep, special words by the healer, or temple services).[36]

If madness is recognizable and diagnosable across all cultures and throughout history, then certainly there exists a clear and objective definition from which to work; it is only logical.

The continued acceptance of the current psychiatric theories of human nature and corresponding systems of "mental health" inevitably depend upon objectively defining mental illness.[37] The muddled and imprecise current definition of madness—which the APA posits—is unsustainable. In large part, psychiatrists' inability or unwillingness to objectively define mental illness stems from their current presuppositional philosophies and the many convoluted beliefs that have arisen in the last century. Yet, as will be unfolded in this chapter, when the peripheral distractions and numerous theories surrounding mental illness are set aside, a precise, consistent, and well-established definition of madness will emerge.

In truth, the claim that madness is a fluid idea that cannot be defined is not an accurate one; there exists a consistent theme

---

[36] Kenneth J. Weiss and the *Group for the Advancement of Psychiatry*, "A Trip Through the History of Psychiatry, *Psychiatric Times Online* (November 7, 2017): http://www.psychiatrictimes.com/blogs/history-psychiatry/trip-through-history-psychiatry?GUID=31158D64-F01A-4DEA-AC1A-D3CE843FC9BC&rememberme=1&ts=14112017.

[37] "Some of this disputatiousness is the hazard of any professional specialty. But when psychiatrists say, as they have during each of these fights, that the success or failure of their efforts could sink the whole profession, they aren't just scoring rhetorical points. The authority of any doctor depends on their ability to name a patient's suffering. For patients to accept a diagnosis, they must believe that doctors know—in the same way that physicists know about gravity or biologists about mitosis—that their disease exists and that they have it. But this kind of certainty has eluded psychiatry, and every fight over nomenclature threatens to undermine the legitimacy of the profession by revealing its dirty secret: that for all their confident pronouncements, psychiatrists can't rigorously differentiate illness from everyday suffering. This is why, as one psychiatrist wrote after the APA voted homosexuality out of the *DSM*, 'There is a terrible sense of shame among psychiatrists, always wanting to show that our diagnoses are as good as the scientific ones used in real medicine'" (Greenberg, "Battle to Define Mental Illness").

throughout history that clearly defines madness. Understanding this historic uniformity of madness is essential not only to define mental illness but also to discover its cause and remedy.

Today's psychiatrists, psychologists, and sociologists tend to explore and theorize about various types of madness while insisting that these allegedly different forms of mental illnesses are physical diseases. In turn, society in general has accepted the notion that there exist types of mental illness rather than believing there is only one concept of madness.

However, from its first recognition, people considered madness to be a singular concept that manifested itself in different ways; there existed only a "unitary psychosis."[38] This traditional view was clearly understood and widely accepted.

Likewise, in the past, societies considered madness to be a religious, spiritual, and social problem rather than a biological or medical issue. Mary Boyle cites the historian Andrew Scull:

> Scull (1979) describes one of these changes as a shift in responsibility for social deviance from the family and local community to a formal and centralized authority. This transition, however, involved much more than the compulsory construction of state asylums. It was accompanied by the transformation of the term 'insanity' from a 'vague, culturally defined phenomenon afflicting an unknown but probably small, proportion of the population into a condition which could only be authoritatively diagnosed, certified and dealt with by a group of legalized experts' (Scull, 1975: 218). The segregation of those labeled insane from society in general and other deviants in particular was therefore contemporaneous with the growth of medical influence over this population and with the emergence of the new specialty of psychiatry.[39]

As the terms to describe madness changed, so too did people's view of the essence of madness, what causes it, who can treat it, and how it is managed.

---

[38] On this idea, see M. Lanczik, "Heinrich Neumann und seine Lehre von der Einheitspsychose," *Fundamenta Psychaitrica* 3 (1989): 49-54.

[39] Mary Boyle, *Schizophrenia: A Scientific Delusion?* 2nd ed. (London: Routledge, 2002), 17-18.

Prior to society's acceptance of psychiatry as a reputable medical field at the end of the eighteenth century,[40] resolving madness and problems of human nature were matters of theology, morality, and philosophy. Madness required pastoral care rather than medical treatment. Former APA president and head of psychiatry at Columbia University Jeffrey Lieberman acknowledges that most all of society once understood madness to be a moral issue and the realm of pastors.[41] Similarly, the historian Roy Porter notes that "the insane were also cared for in religious houses."[42] Psychologist Tana Dineen details this reality further:

> Before the mid-1800s, psychology had been the province of philosophers and theologians, carried out through speculation and inference, intuition and generalization. However, by mid-century, the scientific method, which had shown modest gains in the understanding of physical nature, *began to be applied to human nature* [emphasis added].[43]

In her statement, Dineen raises an important issue: is madness the domain of biological medicine or a problem of human nature? The answer to this question will not only help to define madness; it will also shed light on whether madness is still the domain of pastors and theologians or is now legitimately the practice of psychologists, psychiatrists, and other clinicians.

In truth, today's mental health therapists still engage in pastoral work very similar to that of their religious predecessors; it is just that their doctrines and practices are based in secularism. Psychiatrist Sigmund Freud acknowledges that psychotherapy is pastoral by nature:

---

40 Shorter, *A History of Psychiatry*, 1.

41 Lieberman, *Shrinks*, 30.

42 Roy Porter, *Madness: A Brief History* (New York: Oxford University Press, 2002), 19.

43 Tana Dineen, *Manufacturing Victims: What the Psychology Industry is Doing to People*, 3rd ed. (New York: Robert Davies Multimedia Publishing, 2000), 236.

> The words, 'secular pastoral worker,' might well serve as a general formula for describing the function of the analyst. We do not seek to bring relief by receiving him into the catholic, protestant, or socialist community. *We seek rather to enrich him from his own internal sources* [emphasis added]. . . . Such activity as this is pastoral work in the best sense of the word.[44]

Psychiatrist Peter Breggin comments on how even therapy relates to the soul,

> The word *therapy* comes from the Greek *therapeutikos*, meaning attendant or one who takes care of another, while *psycho* comes from the Greek psyche, meaning soul or being. Psychotherapy means ministering to the soul or being of another. It is psychiatry that has medicalized and corrupted the word to mean "the treatment of mental illness."[45]

Though many forms of counseling and treatment of mental struggles differ in their foundational anthropology and outworking practices, each approach attempts to minister to or guide another's soul toward a restored state. *Madness* and *insanity* were historical terms first framed within the context of theology and philosophy and, more recently, within a medical paradigm.[46]

Not only have humanists introduced a new paradigm by which to interpret madness, but so also, they have replaced the word *madness* with numerous other descriptive phrases and terms.[47] Despite the fact that many people today do not describe human impairment and distress as *madness*, the concept has an important history that is either being ignored or has been forgotten. Understanding this history is essential to defining mental illness objectively.

---

[44] Sigmund Freud, "Postscript to the Question of Lay Analysis," *SE* 20 (1927): 255-56.

[45] Peter R. Breggin, *Toxic Psychiatry* (New York: St. Martin's Press, 1991), 375.

[46] Porter, *Madness*, 185.

[47] The various replacement terms now used by psychiatrists will be examined in chapter three.

It is most beneficial, then, for this study to begin defining insanity by comparing madness from its first concept to how it is perceived and framed now. While it is often obstructed by current theories, constructs, and labels, a precise definition of mental illness does, in fact, exist. However, understanding both the genuine substance of madness and its unchanged nature throughout history will require an examination of these historical bookends.

THE FIRST DEFINITION

From the earliest historical records, madness was a theological concept, and virtually all historians acknowledge that people first considered insanity to be a spiritual/religious matter. The *Group for the Advancement of Psychiatry* explains, "Early civilizations attributed mood thought and behavioral differences to the spirits, gods, and demons."[48] Even as late as the 1940s, many psychiatrists realized that the soul (psyche) was the domain of theologians. For example, in a 1942 article published by the American Psychiatric Association (APA), writers discussed in earnest whether or not "idiots" (those with valid physical impairments) should be euthanized and commented that the innate value of an individual characterized by such physical and mental deformity "is a theological point on which the medical man cannot speak as an expert."[49] In its remarks, the APA also recognized that the soul and brain are not the same and that things related to the soul are not the domain of medicine. This view, of course, has changed.

Despite different theories of causation and suggested remedies that exist today, most historians recognize that the concept of madness is clearly presented in the ancient writing of

---

[48] Group for the Advancement of Psychiatry, "The History of Psychiatry 19th Century."

[49] American Psychiatric Association, "Euthanasia," *American Journal of Psychiatry* vol. 99 (1942): 141.

the Bible. In fact, the most respected historians of madness and psychiatry typically trace the origins of insanity primarily to the Bible and a few other less-prominent religious writings. The works of Edward Shorter, Roy Porter, Petteri Pietikäinen, and Andrew Scull, who all approach madness with praise of the biological perspective of modern psychiatry identify the Holy Scriptures as one of the original and main sources in describing and illustrating madness. For example, psychiatrist Petteri Pietikäinen states in his book *Madness: A History* that "myths and religious stories are the oldest written sources that refer to madness . . . . Judaism, Christianity and madness are closely intertwined."[50] Roy Porter begins his historical account of madness by referencing the Bible:

> Madness may be as old as mankind. . . . Madness figures, usually as a fate or punishment, in early religious myths and in heroic fables. In Deuteronomy (6:5) [sic; Deuteronomy 28:28] it is written, "The Lord will smite thee with madness'; the Old Testament tells of many possessed of devils, and relates how the Lord punished Nebuchadnezzar by reducing him to bestial madness.[51]

Despite believing that Scripture's historical accounts are myths, Porter recognizes the true signs of madness observed in the account of king Nebuchadnezzar. Andrew Scull likewise points to Nebuchadnezzar as one of the premier examples of madness in antiquity, and many other historians claim that this record best represents the biblical concept:

> Swollen with pride at his conquests he boasts of 'the might of my power', only for a voice from heaven to denounce his impiety. Driven mad, he 'did eat grass as oxen, and his body was wet with the dew of heaven, until his hairs were grown like eagle's feathers, and his nails like birds' claws' (PL.2). According to the Bible, seven years later, the curse was removed. His reason returned. His kingship was restored, and he regained his former power and glory.[52]

---

50 Pietikäinen, *Madness*, 16.

51 Porter, *Madness*, 10.

52 Andrew Scull, *Madness in Civilization: A Cultural History of Insanity* (New Jersey: Princeton University Press, 2015), 20.

The account of Nebuchadnezzar is not the summary of madness in Scripture, though. In fact, before examining Nebuchadnezzar, there are important terms and associated concepts in both the Old and New Testaments that illuminate the true biblical definition of madness. These different terms are not different types of insanity; they simply reveal different situations where the unified definition of madness is utilized.

A Reflection of False Beliefs

The term *madness* was first used to label a person who dogmatically believed falsehood or whom others regarded to be deceived. Deception and belief are the core elements of historical madness.

The Biblical Perspective

The Bible not only offers one of the first understandings of madness, but it also provides perspective in its ancient languages. The first Hebrew term translated as *madness* in English is *shiggayon*[53], and it is used six times in the Old Testament—all of which translate into English as *madness* or *insanity*. In 2 Kings 9:8-12, Elisha the prophet sends one of his servants to Jehu to communicate a specific truth from God. Jehu and his servants, though, are unwilling to or incapable of believing God's messenger, and thus Jehu responds to the prophet by judging him to be a "madman":

> When Jehu came out to the servants of his master, they said to him, "Is all well? Why did this mad fellow come to you?" And he said to them, "You know the fellow and his talk." And they said, "That is not true; tell us now." And he said, "Thus and so he spoke to me, saying, 'Thus says the LORD, I anoint you king over Israel.'" (ESV)[54]

In this particular case, the person who had truth was judged as being mad by the one who would not accept truth. But this

---

[53] The Hebrew word for "madman" is *meshugga* (Pietikäinen, *Madness*, 16).

[54] The *ESV* is used throughout this book unless otherwise noted.

account illustrates an important aspect of madness: the one who seemingly lacks truth or is deceived is the person identified as being mad. Of equal importance is the fact that a person's words were an essential diagnostic tool in recognizing madness.

The same Hebrew word (*shiggayon*) is used similarly in Hosea 9:7b: "The prophet is a fool; the man of the spirit is mad, because of your great iniquity and great hatred." Truth is not easily received by those who have pre-existing false beliefs and hold to them with conviction. Jeremiah 29:26-28 utilizes the word in a similar fashion:

> The LORD has made you priest instead of Jehoiada the priest, to have charge in the house of the LORD over every *madman* who prophesies, to put him in the stocks and neck irons. Now why have you not rebuked Jeremiah of Anathoth who is prophesying to you? For he has sent to us in Babylon, saying, "Your exile will be long; build houses and live in them, and plant gardens and eat their produce [emphasis added]."

In all of these biblical passages, the men diagnosed as being mad were in actuality telling the truth; they were all prophets whose messages were considered to be false, unreasonable, unacceptable, or difficult to believe (absurd). In this sense, madness describes someone who is perceived to be detached from truth or reality and is saying and/or doing something that is difficult to reason or is not easily explained within a person's worldview.

In 1 Samuel 21:14-15, disbelief/false faith is also emphasized and further exposes that the one calling another mad may themselves be the one deceived and denying truth. After observing what he believed to be an unfamiliar disabled man at his gate, King Achish turns to his servants and says,

> "Do I lack *madmen*, that you have brought this fellow to behave as a *madman* in my presence? Shall this fellow come into my house?" Then Achish said to his servants, "Behold, you see the man is *mad*. Why then have you brought him to me? [emphasis added]"

The disabled man that Achish saw was King David—who was only pretending to be impaired because of his fear (12-13).[55] Just as those who were deceived and rejected the words of the prophets in 2 Kings 9, Hosea 9, and Jeremiah 29, King Achish had been deceived not by words, but by David's behavior. Herein lies the second diagnostic tool in antiquity for identifying madness: behavior. In each of these aforementioned passages, we see that people in antiquity used a person's words and behavior to interpret whether someone was living in truth or characterized by madness.

Ironically, it is many times the people in Scripture who insist that others are mad, who are themselves the most delusional. For example, in the New Testament, Jesus' words and behavior did not fit what the Jews believed, so these religious men rejected His message and life, judging Him to be deceived to the extent that they believed He was possessed by demons—the

---

[55] The Hebrew word טַעַם (translated as insane in most English versions) in this text means discernment or perception and not madness as we believe it to be today. It is not the same word ("madness") that king Achish used to describe David. In other passages, such as Jeremiah 48:11 and Jonah 3:7, the word means "flavor" or "taste." The text literally states that David changed his behavior to be perceived as someone who had no perception/discernment. To use the word's other meaning, observable amoral behavior is a taste of a person's identity, and moral behavior is a taste of their character. In this particular case, the poor translation of insanity reflects someone who has lost discernment (ability to know between right and wrong) or reason from a physical malady versus someone who does not want to reason—to accept reality. The Bible also utilizes this word to describe what may very well be dementia in Job 12:20: "He deprives the trusted ones of speech and takes away the *discernment* [ability to taste/reason] of the elders (*NASB*)." The *KJV* translates it "taketh away the *understanding* of the aged." Another example of the word's usage is found in 1 Samuel 25:32-33: "Then David said to Abigail, "Blessed be the LORD God of Israel, who sent you this day to meet me, and blessed be your discernment [ability to taste], and blessed be you, who have kept me this day from bloodshed and from avenging myself by my own hand." The term is used specifically here in reference to not murdering ("having shed blood without cause" verse 31). The concept of tasting or discerning is of great importance in Scripture. It is regularly used as a clear metaphor to illuminate human morality/reasoning/ understanding between right/good and wrong/evil. Job 12:11 explains the metaphor specifically: "Does not the ear test words, as the palate tastes its food?" Those who have an ability to taste what is good and bad (observed in both their speech and behavior), must be held accountable for their behavior. David was pretending to be physically impaired rather than manic or mad.

height of being deceived. In their minds, Christ was detached from reality (vs. 46-52): "The Jews answered him, 'Are we not right in saying that you are a Samaritan and have a demon?'" John 10:20-21 discusses the same scenario and sheds further light on the biblical concept of insanity:

> Many of them said, "He has a demon and is insane [*manic*]; why listen to him?" Others said, "These are not the words of one who is oppressed by a demon. Can a demon open the eyes of the blind?"

The Jews diagnosed Christ to be delusional—possessed and manic (μαίνομαι; manic; from where modern psychiatry derives its concept of mania). Christ, who claimed to be an embodiment of truth (John 14:6), was accused of being overtaken by deceit. Herein lies a human tendency and an important factor in identifying madness: when truth does not fit one's ideology or established faith—especially when truth is shocking, horrific, or difficult to understand—people tend to frame the messenger—based upon their words and behavior—as being mad or possessed.

Conversely, if someone is genuinely possessed or given over to deception (manic), then the term *madness* easily explains unbelievable mindsets and behaviors which are out of the ordinary and difficult to understand. Both the claim of demonic possession and madness identify people who are perceived to be deceived—thinking or living apart from established truth or reality. This reality is also in part why many historians falsely summarize the biblical concept of madness as being handed down by gods or demons, and why many cultures continue to consider the mindsets and behaviors assigned to the psychiatric concepts of psychosis, schizophrenia, madness, and mania as demonic possession. Both the Bible's and many societies' correlation between madness and demonic possession and oppression emphasizes deception as the foundational problem of both.

In the New Testament, a clear explanation of madness is also found in Acts 26:24-26. It is in this context that Festus diagnoses

Paul as being mad. As with John 10:20-21, the Greek root word is μανία (mania):

> "And as he was saying these things in his defense, Festus said with a loud voice, "Paul, you are *out of your mind* [manic]; your great learning is driving you *out of your mind* [manic]." But Paul said, "I am not out *of my mind* [manic], most excellent Festus, *but I am speaking true and rational words.* For the king knows about these things, and to him I speak boldly For I am *persuaded* [emphases added].

Paul's words in Acts provide further clarity about the nature of mania. For example, the Bible presents mania as the antithesis of "true and rational words." This statement not only highlights the nature of mania to be deception, it again emphasizes that a person's words provide one of the most important diagnostic tools for identifying madness. Madness, then (according to Scripture) is any seemingly irrational or deceptive mindset observed in a person's words and behaviors.

Another passage where the concept of madness/mania is found is in Acts 12:14-16. The early church had been in earnest prayer that Peter would be released. But as the text reveals, these Christians did not actually believe that he would be. When Peter presented himself at the very house where the Christians were praying for his release, a young girl greeted him at the door. Upon realizing that it was in fact Peter, the girl ran to tell the congregation:

> Recognizing Peter's voice, in her joy she did not open the gate but ran in and reported that Peter was standing at the gate. They said to her, "You are *out of your mind* [manic]." But she kept insisting that it was so, and they kept saying, "It is his angel!" But Peter continued knocking, and when they opened, they saw him and were amazed.

The congregation judged the girl as either being delusional (believing something to be true though it is outside of reality) or as hallucinating (perceiving something to be true though it is outside of sensory reality). Thus, they accused the young girl of being manic or deceived. In actuality, it was the congregation that was delusional and not the girl.

The interactions between Christ and the Jews, between Paul and Festus, and between the young girl and the first century church shed light on what enables madness: faith/belief systems concerning what is true must be in conflict between at least two people. Whoever has the most power or the greatest communal support in determining what is true, then, is given the right to judge others as standing outside of reason. Stated differently, the person or people who seem to possess truth or at least control the concept of truth—especially in relation to human normalcy—are in the position to diagnose others as being mad.

Ironically, in all of these aforementioned scriptural examples, those diagnosed as being mad were in their right minds. Festus' diagnosing Paul with mania, for example, was based upon Festus' own inability to believe Paul's words of truth. Madness in Scripture clearly identifies someone who is perceived to be deceived or who has abandoned reason—the ability to discern what is true or real.

Another Greek term in the Bible that provides further understanding is ἐξίστημι (*existémi*)—thus the English word *existence.* The word *existemi*—meaning to "stand out" or to "appear outside of" could be considered a synonym of mania/madness. When Scripture uses the word in context of someone's beliefs, it conveys the idea of a truth beyond or outside of a person's mental ability to comprehend or accept.

Unbelief, astonishment, and or acceptance of falsehood are common translations of *existemi* in the English versions of Scripture. Mark 3:21 is one illustration: "And when his family heard it, they went out to seize him, for they were saying, "He is out of his mind [*existomi*]."[56] In other words, the observers diagnosed Christ by his words as thinking outside of what they considered to be rational. In this sense, "being out of one's mind" describes someone who is thinking or behaving in a manner that is contrary to the shared beliefs or expected norms.

In modern English people regularly assert that something or someone is crazy, insane, or out of his/her mind when what they observe or hear is hard to believe, comprehend, to reason

---

[56] John 7:5, "For not even his brothers believed him."

about, or is outside of what they consider to be normal or acceptable.[57] People utilize the English terms *mad, crazy,* and *insane* to explain something out of the ordinary, unbelievable, or incomprehensible. Mary Boyle acknowledges that

> by definition, the label 'mad' is applied to those whose behaviour is incomprehensible, who violate social norms in ways which inspire at least bewilderment, if not fear.[58]

When a person's words or behavior elicit fear, are bizarre, or are out of the ordinary, society regularly judges and categorizes such phenomenon as insanity. For example, the man who sees his favorite baseball player hit five homeruns in the same game—an unusual accomplishment to say the least—might later describe the game as "a crazy game," or what the player did as "maddening." A young lady who arrives at baggage claim after a long trip to find her bags missing might express her disbelief by saying, "This is insane; you have got to be kidding me!" The terms for *madness* (e.g., mad, insane, and crazy) work in these situations because they convey unbelief or describe something outside of our ability to rationalize, believe, or accept as true.

A Modern Perspective

Lest the reader believe this concept of madness to only be found in Scripture, it is helpful to observe the same tendency secularists have in diagnosing people who declare inconvenient, uncomfortable, or difficult truths or whose words and behaviors are contrary to popular belief or the established social worldview by observing how many contemporary psychiatrists insist that Jesus Christ—God the Father's messenger—was mad/mentally ill. As with many in antiquity, Jesus' words and behavior do not set well with many of today's secularists who

---

[57] This concept is also expressed in 2 Kings 9:20: "Again the watchman reported, 'He reached them, but he is not coming back. And the driving is like the driving of Jehu the son of Nimshi, for he drives mad [in an unbelievable way].'"

[58] Boyle, *Schizophrenia*, 20.

embrace humanistic beliefs about human nature. Just as the Jews pronounced Christ to be possessed by the deceiver and manic, many psychiatrists have, in retrospect, diagnosed Christ as suffering from psychosis, paranoia, mania, and other alleged forms of mental illness. Take for example the comments of French psychiatrist Charles Binet-Sangle in 1910:

> In short, the nature of the hallucinations of Jesus, as they are described in the orthodox Gospels, permits us to conclude that the founder of the Christian religion was afflicted with religious paranoia.[59]

Similarly, renowned psychiatrist, founding member of the World Psychiatric Association, and former Professor of Psychiatry at Duke University, William Sargant, said in 1974, "Jesus Christ might simply have returned to his carpentry following the use of modern psychiatric treatments."[60] Or consider the diagnosis of several more modern psychiatrists as published in the *Journal of Neuropsychiatry and Clinical Neuroscience* in 2012 and copyrighted by the APA:

> "Jesus' experiences can be potentially conceptualized within the framework of Paranoid Schizophrenia or Psychosis NOS. Other reasonable possibilities might include bipolar and schizoaffective disorders . . . hyperreligiosity." They also point out that Christ most likely had "suicide-by-proxy," described as: "any incident in which a suicidal individual causes his or her death to be carried out by another person. [61]

They also state of other biblical figures,

> The authors have analyzed the religious figures Abraham, Moses, Jesus, and St. Paul from a behavioral, neurologic, and neuropsychiatric perspective to determine whether new insights can be achieved about the nature of their revelations. Analysis reveals that these individuals

---

[59] Charles Binet-Sangle, *The Madness of Jesus* (1910). Quoted in Albert Schweitzer, *The Psychiatric Study of Jesus*, trans. Charles Joy (Orlando: Magnolia, 1911), 44-45.

[60] William Sargant, "The Movement in Psychiatry Away from the Philosophical," *The Times*, August 22, 1974, 14.

[61] Evan D. Murray, Miles G. Cunningham, and Bruce H. Price, "The Role of Psychotic Disorders in Religious History Considered," *Journal of Neuropsychiatry and Clinical Neurosciences* 24 (2012): 410-26.

> had experiences that resemble those now defined as psychotic symptoms, suggesting that their experiences may have been manifestations of primary or mood disorder-associated psychotic disorders. The rationale for this proposal is discussed in each case with a differential diagnosis. Limitations inherent to a retrospective diagnostic examination are assessed. Social models of psychopathology and group dynamics are proposed as explanations for how followers were attracted and new belief systems emerged and were perpetuated. The authors suggest a new *DSM* diagnostic subcategory as a way to distinguish this type of psychiatric presentation. These findings support the possibility that persons with primary and mood disorder-associated psychotic symptoms have had a monumental influence on the shaping of Western civilization. It is hoped that these findings will translate into increased compassion and understanding for persons living with mental illness.[62]

When peoples' beliefs, words, and/or behavior do not fit into our worldview or we cannot seem to rationalize who they are, we tend to view them as mad. If in fact these people are outside of established truth, then they are certainly given over to deception/delusions. But many times, those who are diagnosed as mad simply expose an aspect of human nature that is disturbing, difficult to accept, contrary to common beliefs, and/or hard to explain from the perspective of the observer's worldview.

Harry Eiss explains that madness is something believed to be out of the norm and apart from the physical nature,

> There is nothing at all degrading about being insane, at least not from my perspective. In fact, those deemed insane are perhaps the only ones who fit the category of genius, the artists, shamans, perhaps even saviors, condemned, ridiculed, some confined to institutions, at least one crucified. They are humans of the highest level, the ones who have connected to the mysteries of existence beyond the meaningless physical world of the body, the ones giving us the only maps that really matter, the maps of meaning and value.[63]

A person's faith in what is true—for better or for worse—ultimately forms their definition of madness.

---

[62] Ibid.

[63] Harry Eiss, *Insanity and Genius: Masks of Madness and the Mapping of Meaning and Value*, 2nd ed. (New Castle, England: Cambridge Scholars Publishing, 2008), preface viii.

A Response According to Worldview

We first observed madness to be a description of someone perceived to be living in or speaking out falsehood. Now we learn that it is also an impairing reaction to circumstances, environments, and/or traumatic experiences that rest outside of our faith's ability to bear them.

Since madness depends upon established truth or reality, it is reasonable to conclude that when people are faced with unfortunate, horrific, distressful, or painful realities in their lives, denying reality or attempting to dissociate from it can easily become their response. Denying reality to embrace falsehood is another way in which madness is observed. People's deceptive reactions to adversity or trauma take the form of words and behavior, and though they may vary, the underlying cause remains the same.

All people need to respond to and find explanation for adversity and trauma, and they must do so according to their faith. In this sense, madness explains various responses of people whose faith is unable to explain, let alone bear the weight of, the distressful realities of life. To many, embracing deceit (madness) becomes the only perceived course of endurance and means to explain unbearable truth.

A Biblical Perspective

When life becomes extremely difficult, the human tendency is to respond by turning to falsehood or distorting reality. This understanding represents the biblical definition of madness. In Deuteronomy 28:33-34ff the Bible states,

> A nation that you have not known shall eat up the fruit of your ground and of all your labors, and you shall be only *oppressed* and *crushed* continually, *so that you are driven mad by the sights that your eyes see* [emphasis added].

This text not only helps define madness, it specifically explains what drives people to it: "by the sights that your eyes see." The commentator John Gill remarks,

> On account of the shocking things seen by them, their dreadful calamities, oppressions, and persecutions, such as before related; not only violent diseases on their bodies, which were grievous to behold, as well as their pains were intolerable, and made them mad.[64]

A person's faith must be able to explain and respond to the real and anticipated distressful experiences of life, but when an individual is being "crushed" (to be made hopeless, unable to escape bondage, weighted beyond ability)[65] or "oppressed" (to be deceived or defrauded),[66] the need to think and react according to truth is vital. But, unfortunately, it is a common human tendency to turn to deceit as a defense mechanism.

The Bible, and not psychiatry, first described the normal human response to distress and trauma that is now regularly referred to as post-traumatic stress disorder (PTSD) within psychiatric theory. But Scripture does not present this reaction as a disorder or an abnormality; it reveals post-traumatic stress to be a normal and expected human response to tragedy. In Ecclesiastes 7:7, King Solomon states it as such: "Surely oppression drives the wise [those who possess knowledge] into madness." When people experience trauma that rests outside of their ability to mentally handle the enormity of the stress, it should be expected ("surely") that they will struggle mentally to resolve these horrific realities and are prone to turn to deception. This reality may be why Gilbert K. Chesterton once said,

---

[64] John Gill, *Commentary on Deuteronomy 28:28-33*, kindle ed.

[65] Judges 10:8 says, "And they *crushed* and oppressed the people of Israel that year. For eighteen years they oppressed all the people of Israel who were beyond the Jordan in the land of the Amorites, which is in Gilead [emphasis added]." Likewise, Isaiah 58:6 states, "Is not this the fast that I choose: to loose the bonds of wickedness, to undo the straps of the yoke, to let the *oppressed* go free, and to break every yoke [emphasis added]?" Being crushed is finding yourself in a hopeless situation out of your control; it is bondage.

[66] Deuteronomy 24:14 "You shall not *oppress* a hired worker who is poor and needy, whether he is one of your brothers or one of the sojourners who are in your land within your towns [emphasis added]." Leviticus 19:13 also says, "You shall not *oppress* your neighbor or rob him. The wages of a hired worker shall not remain with you all night until the morning [emphasis added]."

> Imagination does not breed insanity. *Exactly what does breed insanity is reason* [emphasis added]. Poets do not go mad; but chess-players do. Mathematicians go mad, and cashiers; but creative artists very seldom. I am not, as will be seen, in any sense attacking logic: I only say that this danger does lie in logic, not in imagination.[67]

When truth is too much to bear, deception—rejecting reality—becomes a common coping mechanism. Madness does not expose an abnormality but does affirm the shared fragility of all human nature.

If our faith is not established in truth—it is a false belief, then being hopeless, powerless, or deeply hurt can cause us to further embrace deceit by distorting or denying reality. When people endure trauma or their actions produce guilt and their faith is unable to rationalize such a reality, then that person must either change his/her worldview or find a way to disassociate from the overwhelming circumstances. Stated differently, when our perspective and reality do not fit together, one or the other must bend in attempt to resolve the ensuing mental turmoil.

But Scripture not only establishes the normalcy of madness as a reaction to trauma, it also touches on how those who "oppress"/defraud others can themselves be driven mad by their own horrific mindsets, behaviors, and guilt. Judas Iscariot[68] illustrates well how false fixed beliefs can progress and lead to destructive behavior when faced with unbearable truth. Judas was an accountant (John 12:6), who falsely believed that money and power would bring him satisfaction (Matthew 26:14). But soon after betraying Jesus for personal financial gain, he realized that blood money and power were false hopes and thus false beliefs. Coupled with guilt, the weight of what Judas had done in rejecting Christ was too much for his mind to bear, and Judas, instead of turning from destructive deceit and embracing truth,

---

[67] Gilbert K. Chesterton, *Orthodoxy* (London: John Lane, 1908): http://www.freeclassicebooks .com/Chesterton,%20G.%20K/Orthodoxy.pdf.

[68] Iscariot means "the false one" or "deceiver" (Joan E. Taylor, "The Name 'Iskarioth' (Iscariot)," *Journal of Biblical Literature* 129 no. 2 [Summer 2010]: 369).

reacted to the torment of reality by committing suicide (Matthew 27:3-10):

> Then when Judas, his betrayer, saw that Jesus was condemned, he changed his mind and brought back the thirty pieces of silver to the chief priests and the elders, saying, "I have sinned by betraying innocent blood." They said, "What is that to us? See to it yourself." And throwing down the pieces of silver into the temple, he departed, and he went and hanged himself. But the chief priests, taking the pieces of silver, said, "It is not lawful to put them into the treasury, since it is blood money." So they took counsel and bought with them the potter's field as a burial place for strangers. Therefore that field has been called the Field of Blood to this day. Then was fulfilled what had been spoken by the prophet Jeremiah, saying, "And they took the thirty pieces of silver, the price of him on whom a price had been set by some of the sons of Israel, and they gave them for the potter's field, as the Lord directed me."

Judas's false perceptions of reality led not only to the betrayal of his rabbi and friend but also to his eventual suicide. His story illustrates that rejecting truth can have disastrous ripple effects for the deceived and for those around them.

The Modern Perspective

More and more contemporary clinicians are coming to the conclusion that constructs of mental illness represent common but impairing reactions to events and environments which people are unable to mentally bear. Psychiatrist R. D. Laing wrote in 1967 that "behavior that gets labeled schizophrenia is a special strategy that a person invented in order to live in an unlivable situation."[69] Similarly, Alfred Adler described what he believed to be severe (psychosis) and milder (neurosis) forms of madness: "Neurosis and psychosis are modes of expression for human beings who have lost courage."[70] Likewise, renowned psychiatrist Arthur Kleinman once stated that psychiatrist's

---

[69] R.D. Laing, *The Politics of Experience and the Bird of Paradise (*England: Penguin, 1967,) 115.

[70] Alfred Adler quoted by Jane Griffith and Robert L. Powers, *The Lexicon of Adlerian Psychology*, 2nd ed. (Port Townsend, WA: Adlerian Psychology Associates, 2007), 20.

primary job does not concern biology but rather a person's history:

> Most of psychiatric care is not about the determination of brain pathology or the choice of a particular drug to cure the patient's disease, though these activities are not unimportant. *The psychiatrist's work is chiefly about people's life stories. It is about aspirations and defeats, about passions and tragedies; in other words, it has to do with the deeply personal and life world (family, work, and school) problems that constitute the neuroses* [emphasis added].[71]

If reality or truth cannot be explained within a person's worldview (a presuppositional belief system by which one interprets all of life), then either changing those fundamental beliefs or detaching one's self from reality and embracing deception are the only two choices. That mental strategy/mode of expression, which Scripture explains and Laing, Adler, Kleinman and numerous others recognize, is a false belief system.

Many modern secular clinicians understand that schizophrenia, bipolar, paranoia, and other forms of psychosis and mania are regularly the result of experiences not being resolved or making sense within a person's preconceived beliefs about oneself, life, and others around him/her. In fact, the first edition of the *DSM* (*DSM-I)* posited various manifestations of madness as "schizophrenic reaction," "manic-depressive reaction," and "conversion reaction," to name a few.[72] Until recent history, most psychiatrists understood madness to be a reaction to life's adversity.

Today's psychiatric bible, the *DSM-5,* still recognizes in its imprecise definition of mental illness that distress and impairment are correlates: "Mental disorders are usually associated with significant distress or disability in social,

---

[71] Arthur Kleinman, *Rethinking Psychiatry: From Cultural Category to Personal Experience* (New York: Free Press, 1988), 139-40.

[72] Shorter, *A History of Psychiatry,* 299.

occupational, or other important activities."[73] The *DSM-5* also states that

> distress may take the form of hallucinations or pseudo-hallucinations and overvalued ideas that may present clinically similar to true psychosis but are normative to the patient's subgroup.[74]

Though an objective explanation of what differentiates "pseudo-hallucinations" from "true psychosis" has never been offered, madness is still imprecisely defined in the *DSM-5* as a response to trauma or distress. Even in personality disorders, for example, the *DSM*-5 recognizes that "psychosocial stressors may precipitate brief periods of psychotic symptoms."[75]

Many prominent psychiatrists and other mental illness theorists today understand this truth and are slowly changing their beliefs to better agree with empirical evidence. Take for example, one of the most highly regarded researchers on psychosis/schizophrenia, psychiatrist Robin Murray:

> I expect to see the end of the concept of schizophrenia soon. Already the evidence that it is a discrete entity rather than just the severe end of psychosis has been fatally undermined. Furthermore, the syndrome is already beginning to breakdown, for example, into *those cases caused by copy number variations, drug abuse, social adversity, etc* [emphasis added]. Presumably this process will accelerate, and the term *schizophrenia* will be confined to history, like 'dropsy.'[76]

What Murray recognizes[77] is that we all not only respond differently to life's difficulties, but we also experience different circumstances that can lead to similar responses. Some people turn to deep deception in attempt to escape reality, but we all

---

[73] APA, *DSM-5,* 20.

[74] Ibid., 103.

[75] Ibid., 96.

[76] Robin M. Murray, "Mistakes I Have Made in My Research Career," *Schizophrenia Bulletin Online* (December 2016): sbw165. doi: 10.1093/schbul/sbw165.

[77] The claim of "copy number variations" or the gene theory of psychosis will be examined in chapter four.

find identity and protection in what we believe. Psychiatrist Lawrie Reznek explains,

> We also cling to beliefs if they provide comfort and protect us from the terror we experience when we think of our place in the universe. As one group of psychologists put it, we need "a protective shield designed to control the potential for terror that results from awareness of the horrifying possibility that we humans are merely transient animals groping to survive in a meaningless universe, destined only to die and decay." We are attracted to beliefs that are reassuring and that reduce our anxiety about our place in the world. We are more likely to cling to beliefs that reduce our angst about the world than beliefs that have no anxiety-reducing function. . . . Such beliefs are protective—they allow us to not face the difficult question of our mortality and our ultimate insignificance, and thereby protect us against anxiety and the threat of meaninglessness. . . .[78]

In secular terminology, the inability or refusal to accept reality—especially when it is distressful—and turn to deception is regularly called *dissociation*,[79] and people's natural inability to deal with being "crushed" and "oppressed" explains many people's diagnoses of the psychiatric constructs of schizophrenia, bipolar, PTSD, dissociative identity disorder, and dozens of the most prominent constructs of madness known today as mental illnesses. Neurologist Oliver Sacks comments, "The concept of dissociation would seem crucial not only to understanding conditions like hysteria or multiple personality disorder [now called dissociative identity disorder] but also to the understanding of post-traumatic-syndromes."[80] He also states about schizophrenia specifically,

> The hallucinations often experienced by people with schizophrenia also demand a separate consideration, a book of their own, for they

---

78 Reznek, *Delusions and Madness of the Masses*, 61-62.

79 Robert Jay Lifton, *The Nazi Doctors: Medical Killing and the Psychology of Genocide* (New York: Basic Books, 1986), 419. For further study on dissociation, see Daniel R. Berger II, *Mental Illness: The Influence of Nurture* (Taylors, SC: Alethia International Publications, 2016), 73-95.

80 Oliver Sacks, *Hallucinations* (New York: Random House, 2012), 241.

> cannot be divorced from the often profoundly altered inner life and life circumstances of those with schizophrenia.[81]

One recent article in the *Psychiatric Times* remarks on the empirical evidence that consistently correlates traumatic life experiences with today's psychiatric concepts of depression and mania (bipolar disorders): "Bipolar disorder has been linked to traumatic childhood experience and to the potential for violence."[82] But it is not merely childhood trauma that pushes people to embrace deceit. Singer Connie Francis shares how, after being raped in 1974, her ongoing distress led her to be diagnosed as having bipolar disorder:

> I know something about PTSD. While I was on tour in New York in 1974, I was raped at knifepoint in a motel. It was terrifying. I spent two and a half hours negotiating for my life. After that, I couldn't' sleep. I saw the attacker's face everywhere. I was hospitalized; they thought I had bipolar illness. I took lithium, but all it did was keep me lying on a couch.[83]

Dr. Charles Whitfield explains this common human tendency to embrace falsehood in order to make sense of life events which our worldview cannot explain,

> If we habitually dissociate because of our childhood trauma, we may feel as though we have lost the "point of contact" with our inner and outer reality [spiritual and physical]. We often feel "out of touch," with the present moment, "artificial," or as though we are "playing, acting . . ." We may dissociate our awareness and experience in any of several of our life areas—the physical, mental, emotional, and spiritual. [84]

---

[81] Ibid., preface xiii.

[82] Allison M. R. Lee, Igor I. Galynker, Irina Kopeykina, Hae-Joon Kim, and Tasnia Khatun, "Violence in Bipolar Disorder," *Psychiatric Times Online* (December 16, 2014): http://www.psychiatrictimes.com/bipolar-disorder/violence-bipolar-disorder?GUID=31158D64-F01A-4DEA-AC1A-D3CE843FC9BC&rememberme=1&ts=21042017.

[83] Connie Francis, "When Warriors Come Home," *AARP The Magazine*, December 2017/January 2018, 61.

[84] Charles L. Whitfield, *The Truth about Mental Illness: Choices for Healing* (Deerfield Beach, FL: Health Communications, 2004), 57-58.

Whitfield later comments, "The accumulated research data indicate that a history of repeated child abuse is significantly correlated with psychosis in general, and schizophrenia in particular."[85] Likewise, neurologist V.S. Ramachandran states,

> Psychological defenses in normal people are especially puzzling because at first glance they seem detrimental to survival. Why would it enhance my survival to cling tenaciously to false beliefs about myself and the world?[86]

Truth is not only stranger than fiction, but it is often more difficult to accept. It is understandable then, that the APA would recognize that hallucinations (false sensory perceptions) are also common with post-traumatic stress: "Posttraumatic stress disorder may include flashbacks that have a hallucinatory quality, and hypervigilance may reach paranoid proportions."[87] Former associative justice of the U.S. Supreme Court Oliver Wendell Holmes also recognized that insanity is a person's understanding that he/she cannot mentally bear a truth/reality:

> Insanity is often the logic of an accurate mind overtasked. Good mental machinery ought to break its own wheels and levers, if anything is thrust among them suddenly which tends to stop them or reverse their motion. A weak mind does not accumulate force enough to hurt itself; stupidity often saves a man from going mad."[88]

When reality can no longer be denied, yet it is too much to mentally shoulder, "false fixed belief" or deception becomes the most natural and seemingly logical escape. Journalist Watters and sociologist Ofshe comment on the need to explain a person's thoughts and experiences which do not fit into his/her worldviews:

---

[85] Ibid., 171.

[86] V.S. Ramachandran and Sandra Blakeslee, *Phantoms in the Brain: Probing the Mysteries of the Human Mind* (New York: William Morrow and Company, 1998), 133.

[87] APA, *DSM-5*, 104.

[88] Oliver Wendell Holmes Sr., *Autocrat of the Breakfast Table,*1858 (Reprint, New York: Cosimo, 2005), 38.

> The need to have a mythology to explain our circumstances is greatest when those circumstances are unchangeable mystery. To put it another way: We most desperately need an explanation for a condition like depression when we repeatedly experience it without any ability to escape its deadening symptoms.[89]

In trying to explain their own lives, people tend to utilize deception. Psychiatrist Petteri Pietikäinen states,

> Nobody is born insane. The mad, the mentally ill, the insane were, in most cases, not destined to lose their minds. If their lives had taken different paths, most of them might not have been burdened with mental illness.[90]

Insanity, then, is not an abnormality, but a reaction to truth/ reality that seemingly has no resolution or is unbearable within one's worldview.

Therefore, it is likely that many who are said to be mad are merely dealing with an inconvenient, impairing, or seemingly unbearable truth in ways that are unpopular or uncomfortable for the rest of society. Interestingly enough, the *DSM-5* specifically states that many of its posited disorders are merely cultural concepts of distress:

> *Cultural concepts of distress* refers to ways that cultural groups experiences, understand, and communicate suffering, behavioral problems, or troubling thoughts and emotions. . . . *The current formulation acknowledges that all forms of distress are locally shaped, including the DSM disorders. From this perspective, many DSM diagnoses can be understood as operationalized prototypes that started out as cultural syndromes, and become widely accepted as a result of their clinical and research utility.* Across groups there remain culturally patterned difference in symptoms, ways of talking about distress, and locally perceived causes, which are in turn *associated with coping strategies and patterns of help seeking.* [emphases added][91]

Even from the contemporary psychiatric perspective, mental illness is a state in which people do not know how to or are unable to handle truths about themselves or life's unfortunate

---

[89] Watters and Ofshe, *Therapy's Delusions*, 241, 245.

[90] Pietikäinen, *Madness*, 2.

[91] APA, *DSM-5*, 758.

realities within their worldview; their reactions are "coping strategies." The various labels and theories assigned to different reactions to life's distresses are not different types of madness; they are simply different responses.

People who are deceived, though, are not entirely detached from reality. In fact, a delusion's and a hallucination's content is typically reflective of the person's past traumatic and seemingly unbearable experience or guilt from poor personal choices. Clinical psychologist Richard Bentall recognizes that the content of a delusion (within the concept of psychosis) is always a reflection of a reality that a person wishes to deny or eliminate:

> Delusional ideas rarely lack a nugget of truth. No matter how bizarre the ideas expressed by patients, it is usually possible to identify events in their lives that have contributed to their content. Most often these false beliefs are the result of poor relationships with God or other people.[92]

One common delusion experienced by those who are labeled as psychotic is that aliens created the world and are coming for them; the APA calls these "persecutory delusions."[93] This false fixed belief is not meaningless; it often reflects the person's denial of or dissociation from God and fear of being judged. Others feel guilty about cheating on their spouse and have recurring delusions that a famous actor is in love with them. These delusions are so common that the *DSM-5* has given them the name "erotomanic delusions."[94]

Hallucinations offer the same insight. Many survivors of assault mentally replace their abuser's face with an innocent child's or a demon, and some out of fear of failing God hear God's voice audibly tell them every choice they should make. Others struggle with fear of judgment and guilt from their past

---

[92] Richard Bentall, *Madness Explained: Psychosis and Human Nature* (New York: Penguin, 2003), 308.

[93] APA, *DSM-5*, 87.

[94] Ibid.

sins and mentally transform their unbearable fears and guilt into seemingly visible demons and vivid nightmares.

Though beliefs and perceptions are clearly false, they are regularly metaphors that expose something about the individual, and often they point to trauma or guilt:

> By definition, delusions are false firm ideas that cannot be corrected by reasoning and are out of keeping with patient's educational and cultural background. Delusions can also be regarded as a mode of adaptation to stress and may serve a metaphorical or allegorical function in which the patient portrays her problems and experiences.[95]

Though delusions are false, they still reflect a person's history, relationships, or character. Richard Bentall comments,

> Invariably, psychotic complaints reflect concerns about the self, or relationships with other people. Psychotically depressed people, for example, often believe that they are inadequate, or guilty of imaginary misdeeds. Manic patients, in contrast, often feel that they are superior to others, and are capable of achievements that will amaze the world. The delusional beliefs usually attributed to schizophrenia are particularly redolent with social themes. Patients rarely profess bizarre ideas about animals or inanimate objects. Instead they believe that they are being persecuted by imaginary conspiracies, that they have been denied recognition for inventing the helicopter or the pop-up toaster, that they are loved by pop stars or by their doctors, or that their partners are conducting numerous affairs despite compelling evidence to the contrary.[96]

The same is true for hallucinations; they reveal a person's history and/or character. Psychiatrists Stephen Soreff and George McNeil explain,

> Wish fulfillment creates and propels the hallucinatory experience. Freud made reference to the wish-derived quality and function of the false perception. The hallucination represents an unconscious wish, striving or hope. . . . Hallucinations provide a method to momentarily restore a loss.[97]

---

[95] Tarun Yadav, Yatan Pal Singh Balhara, and Dinesh Kumar Kataria, "Pseudocyesis Versus Delusion of Pregnancy: Differential Diagnoses to be Kept in Mind," *Indian Journal of Psychological Medicine* 34, no. 1 (Jan.-Mar. 2012): 82–84.

[96] Bentall, *Madness Explained*, 203-204.

[97] Stephen M. Soreff and George N. McNeil, *Handbook of Psychiatric Differential Diagnosis* (Littleton, MA: PSG Publishing, 1987), 168.

Chair of the *DSM-IV* task force Allen Frances also remarks about auditory hallucinations,

> [Many clinicians] believe that voices have psychological meaning. And so of course do I. The content, tone, and type of voice can usually shed great and valuable light on the person's fears, impulses, conflicts, perceptions, and attitudes.[98]

The person labeled as mad or psychotic deals with truths/realities that are uncomfortable, impairing, unbearable, undesirable, horrific, or inconvenient by turning to self-deception. At the same time, truths that are deemed necessary or are desirable to the one categorized as mad are still embraced (e.g., stealing food in order to resolve hunger). This "splitting of the mind" is precisely why false fixed beliefs and false sensory perceptions were eventually framed by psychiatrists as "schizophrenia." Peter Breggin, former professor at Harvard Medical School of Psychiatry and full-time consultant for the National Institute of Mental Health (NIMH), describes schizophrenia/psychosis:

> Is there such a thing as schizophrenia? Yes and no. Yes, there are people *who think irrationally* at times and who attribute their problems to seemingly inappropriate causes, such as extraterrestrials or voices in the air. Yes, there are people who think they are God or the devil and repeat the claim no matter how much trouble it gets them into. But no, these people are not biologically defective or inherently different from the rest of us. They are not afflicted with a brain disorder or disease.[99]

Breggin goes on to say about those labeled as schizophrenic,

> They are undergoing a *pscyhospiritual crisis*, usually surrounding issues of basic identity and shame, and typically with feelings of outrage and overwhelm. *They communicate in metaphors that often hint at the heart of*

---

[98] Allen Frances, "Reconciling, Recovery, and Psychiatry: Response to Open Letter, Finding the Right Balance," *Psychology Today Online* (September 15, 2013): https://www.psychologytoday.com/blog/saving-normal/201309/reconciling-recovery-and-psychiatry-response-open-letter.

[99] Breggin, *Toxic Psychiatry*, 45.

> *their problems.* The only reason to call them schizophrenic is to justify the psychiatric establishment and its treatments. [emphases added][100]

A person's psychospiritual crisis often leads that individual to turn to deception and create a psychospiritual metaphor in attempt to ease the burden of reality.

What is also fascinating is how the father of today's modern psychiatric paradigm and psychosis, Emil Kraepelin, realized that a person's delusions and hallucinations—even when revealed through valid physical illnesses—primarily expose a person's spiritual heart (their desires):

> It seems absurd to propose that neurosyphilis [damage to the brain that occurs in the final stages of a syphilitic infection] causes patients to believe that they are the proud possessors of cars, mansions or millions of pounds, and that cocaine causes visual hallucinations of mites and lice. *Rather, the general desires of such people are reflected in their delusions of grandeur* [emphasis added].[101]

What Kraepelin acknowledges is profoundly important to understand: delusions and hallucinations are regularly a part of valid illnesses and physical impairment, but false beliefs and perceptions are never caused by illness. The actual content of false beliefs and misperceptions of life are born out of each person's character and desires and not their physical nature. Trauma, illnesses, and even drugs do not create delusions; they expose the true content of the spiritual heart and the true nature of the individual to be deceived. Dr. Bentall comments,

> The problem, as Kraepelin now saw it, was that the patient's symptoms are not uniquely determined by the disease process. *Rather, the symptoms brought out by the disease depend on the individual nature of the patient* [emphasis added]. These kinds of influences, Kraepelin believed, could be revealed by the methods of comparative psychiatry, which allowed the varying manifestations of a disorder to be studied in different people and different circumstances. Studies of this kind revealed that symptoms were affected by personal and social factors such as sex ('women show a greater propensity to erotic delusions and are less flamboyant in the presentation of delusions of grandeur'), age

---

100 Ibid., 46.

101 Emil Kraepelin, "Clinical Manifestations of Mental Illness," *History of Psychiatry* 3 (1920): 499-529.

('the clinical form of juvenile dementia praecox is ... characterized by occasional excitement on a background of apathy').[102]

A patient's character and history cannot be disconnected from his or her hallucinations and delusions.

Neuroscientific studies also reveal that hearing voices is not an abnormal experience:

> Estimates suggest that we spend at least a quarter of our lives listening to our own inner speech. . . . We all hear voices in our heads. Perhaps the problem arises when our brain is unable to tell that we are the ones producing them.[103]

What if, however, the brain is not causing the false perspective as is speculated? Rather, what if the person who is hallucinating in such a way to be diagnosed as psychotic is simply unwilling to accept the reality that the hallucinations reveal; they deny their own character and/or history, and/or they deny that the voices and thoughts are their own. Psychiatrist Lawrie Reznek also notes that false beliefs should be translated,

> Someone can be pervasively mad, in the sense that most of his beliefs are false. We can understand such a person. As long as there is a bridgehead of observational beliefs that are not in error, we can get translation off the ground.[104]

Every false belief and perception expressed through a behavior reveals a truth about that person's character or history which must be understood.

In accordance, the APA has it wrong; it insists that the content of a delusion (whether bizarre, erotomanic, grandiose, mood-congruent, persecutory, somatic etc.)[105] and hallucinations reveals various types of madness. But Kraepelin and countless

---

[102] Bentall, *Madness Explained,* 17.

[103] Thomas J. Whitford, Bradley N. Jack, Daniel Pearson, Oren Griffiths, David Luque, Anthony W. F. Harris, Kevin M. Spencer, and Mike E. Le Pelley, "Neurophysiological Evidence of Efference Copies to Inner Speech," *eLife Sciences,* December 4, 2017, http://dx.doi.org/10.7554/eLife.28197.

[104] Reznek, *Delusions and Madness of the Masses*, 20.

[105] APA, *DSM-5*, 819-20.

others recognize that a delusion's and a hallucination's content expose a person's character, circumstances, and history. The beliefs and behavior known as *mania* in the *DSM-5*, for example, do not identify a person as bipolar. Instead, beliefs and behaviors expose a person's character and history by bringing the heart's desires to light. Every false belief and perception carries with it a truth about the person who holds it.

Whether from a biblical or secular vantage point, madness represents a person's negative reaction to a truth that rests outside of his/her ability to explain, resolve, and endure. Mental illness is not created by outward pressures or stressors; rather, a person's false fixed beliefs (their desires, fears, guilt, pain etc.) are exposed during these traumatic events. If a person is unwilling to change his/her false beliefs when his/her faith cannot explain inconvenient truth or horrific realities, then deception must be embraced, and by this definition, such a person is mad.

A Result of False Belief

What if people, instead of refusing to accept truth, are incapable of believing it? What if madness is, in many cases, a person's inability to spiritually discern truth? In theological terms, this reality is expressed as human depravity—one's natural condition of spiritual blindness and moral failure that inhibits an individual from understanding and receiving moral truth. In secular ideology, the inability of someone to accept or live in truth—one's spiritual blindness or "false fixed belief"—is explained through the concept of bio-determinism. More specifically, secularists assert both a nature and nurture argument as explanatory of not only what causes madness but what hinders people from seeing and accepting truth.

A Biblical Perspective

Scripture depicts madness as both a rejection of and a reaction to difficult truth, but it also explains false fixed belief (delusions) or deception to explain normal human nature. In other words, Scripture presents every person as deeply impaired with false beliefs, and left to one's self, people are incapable of understanding and accepting moral truth.

According to the Bible, any false faith that opposes or dismisses God's natural or supernatural truths has devastating consequences. But pride—the greatest false belief/delusion—causes the most damage. Proverbs 16:18 explains, "Pride goes before destruction, and a haughty spirit before a fall." If a person's pride keeps him/her from accepting God's truth, then that person has chosen deception and destruction. This is precisely why Scripture consistently correlates madness with pride. In Deuteronomy 28:15, as one illustration, God gave the Jewish people a choice to believe and live out God's truths or embrace deception. Both choices yielded different consequences:

> "But it shall come about, if you do not obey the LORD your God, to observe to do all His commandments and His statutes with which I charge you today, that all these curses will come upon you and overtake you."

In the following verses, several curses or negative consequences are listed for those who in natural pride choose to reject God's truth. In Deuteronomy 28:28-29 one of the consequences listed is madness:

> The LORD will strike you with *madness* and blindness and confusion of mind, and you shall grope at noonday, as the blind grope in darkness, and you shall not prosper in your ways. And you shall be only oppressed and robbed continually, and there shall be no one to help you [emphasis added].

In this context, madness is synonymous with spiritual blindness and confusion of mind, and it is the direct consequence of rejecting God's truths. Blindness is the inability to see, and this metaphor highlights humanity's natural inability to see spiritual truths apart from God's illumination (1 Corinthians 1:8-16). Here again, the Bible defines madness as the rejection of truth or spiritual blindness.

The Bible offers several examples of nations and individuals who in their pride rejected God's truth and falsely trusted in their own wisdom. Zechariah 12:1-5 is one illustration:

> The oracle of the word of the Lord concerning Israel: Thus declares the Lord, who stretched out the heavens and founded the earth and formed the spirit of man within him: "Behold, I am about to make Jerusalem a cup of staggering to all the surrounding peoples. The siege of Jerusalem will also be against Judah. On that day I will make Jerusalem a heavy stone for all the peoples. All who lift it will surely hurt themselves. And all the nations of the earth will gather against it. On that day, declares the Lord, I will strike every horse with panic, and its rider with *madness*. But for the sake of the house of Judah I will keep my eyes open, when I strike every horse of the peoples with blindness.

The Bible presents a reality that if people ignore or reject God and His truth, then they are spiritually blind. Scripture also sets forth that all people are by nature spiritually blinded (Romans 1) and that madness (given over to deceit) is a consequence.

It is likewise helpful at this point to explore the illustration of Nebuchadnezzar that is also so often incorrectly used by historians to summarize the biblical understanding of madness. Scripture emphasizes that it was Nebuchadnezzar's pride—false faith in one's self—that caused him to become delusional/ detached from reality and behave like a cow. Daniel 4:27-33 says,

> Therefore, O king, let my counsel be acceptable to you: break off your sins by practicing righteousness, and your iniquities by showing mercy to the oppressed, that there may perhaps be a lengthening of your prosperity." All this came upon King Nebuchadnezzar. At the end of twelve months he was walking on the roof of the royal palace of Babylon, and the king answered and said, "Is not this great Babylon, which I have built by my mighty power as a royal residence and for the glory of my majesty?" While the words were still in the king's mouth, there fell a voice from heaven, "O King Nebuchadnezzar, to you it is spoken: The kingdom has departed from you, and you shall be driven from among men, and your dwelling shall be with the beasts of the field. And you shall be made to eat grass like an ox, and seven periods of time shall pass over you, until you know that the Most High rules the kingdom of men and gives it to whom he will." Immediately the word was fulfilled against Nebuchadnezzar. He was driven from among men and ate grass like an ox, and his body was wet with the dew of heaven till his hair grew as long as eagles' feathers, and his nails were like birds' claws.

The text (4:34-36) also records how Nebuchadnezzar was restored to a right mind—how his deceitful condition was remedied:

> *At the end of the days I, Nebuchadnezzar, lifted my eyes to heaven, and my reason returned to me, and I blessed the Most High,* and praised and honored him who lives forever, for his dominion is an everlasting dominion, and his kingdom endures from generation to generation; all the inhabitants of the earth are accounted as nothing, and he does according to his will among the host of heaven and among the inhabitants of the earth; and none can stay his hand or say to him, "What have you done?" *At the same time my reason returned to me, and for the glory of my kingdom, my majesty and splendor returned to me.* My counselors and my lords sought me, and I was established in my kingdom, and still more greatness was added to me. [emphases added]

According to Nebuchadnezzar's own testimony, it was his change of mind about his nature and relationship to God that permitted his mind to be restored; he took his eyes off of self and instead turned to God; his spiritual blindness was remedied. The biblical term for changing one's mind from prideful deception to God's truth is *repentance*, and the scriptural word for the mindset required to turn from false faith that is pride to accepting reality about one's self is *humility*. Humility is simply acceptance about the reality of who we really are in relation to God and others.

Nebuchadnezzar's story is unique in that pride does not drive everyone to behave like an animal—though some are deceived to the extent that they also live in a similar condition. While it may be an exceptional story in history, the account of Nebuchadnezzar reveals each person's common human nature; we all naturally but falsely think more highly of ourselves then we should, and this tendency brings with it destructive and impairing consequences. It is no wonder then that Romans 12:1-4 connects renewing the mind with having a true opinion of oneself:

> Do not be conformed to this world, but be transformed by the renewal of your mind, that by testing you may discern what is the will of God, what is good and acceptable and perfect. For by the grace given to me *I say to everyone among you not to think of himself more highly than he ought to think, but to think with sober judgment*, each according to the measure of faith that God has assigned [emphasis added].

This New Testament text makes it clear that in order to behave rightly, a person must have right mindsets. The passage also asserts that the first mindset that each person who has accepted God's truth must change is the false fixed belief about one's own nature or character (pride).

Another New Testament passage which brings further lucidity to the idea of madness being a common human mental state is Romans 1:16-32:

> *For the wrath of God is revealed from heaven against all ungodliness and unrighteousness of men, who by their unrighteousness suppress the truth. . . . For although they knew God, they did not honor him as God or give thanks to him, but they became futile in their thinking, and their foolish hearts were darkened.* Claiming to be wise, they became fools, and exchanged the glory of the immortal God for images resembling mortal man and birds and animals and creeping things.

This passage describes the fall of Adam and Eve in the garden and every person thereafter; it is intended to be a concise anthropology that will be further explained throughout the book of Romans.

A Modern Perspective

What contemporary psychiatrists describe in their many constructs of mental illnesses are varied mindsets and behaviors which are mostly reflective of false fixed beliefs. The *DSM*-5 regularly describes madness using the term *psychosis*, which mainly consists of delusions, hallucinations, and "odd" speech and behavior. But one of the common delusions found in both the constructs of schizophrenia and bipolar disorders—considered to be the most severe forms of madness—is referred to as "grandiose delusions." The APA does not utilize the term *pride*; it prefers the phrases *grandiose delusions* or *delusions of grandeur.*[106] The *DSM* defines the term as "a delusion of inflated worth, power, knowledge, identity or special relationship to a

---

[106] APA, *DSM-5*, 87.

deity or famous person."[107] The *DSM* also notes that grandiosity is a "broad personality trait":

> Believing that one is superior to others and deserves special treatment; self-centeredness; feelings of entitlement; condescension toward others. Grandiosity is a facet of the broad personality trait domain *ANTAGONISM*.[108]

Grandiosity, "self-centeredness," or a haughty spirit/pride (as Scripture calls it) is a false fixed belief about one's own character.

Many of the concepts of madness found in the *DSM* reflect this specific false belief. Individuals labeled as bipolar, for example, are those who psychiatrists have identified as having an exalted and overconfident false opinion of themselves. In fact, clinical studies consistently show that the majority of people labeled as having bipolar disorder express delusions of grandeur.[109] Emil Kraepelin—who is the most significant individual in defining a modern secular perspective of madness and is largely responsible for creating the construct of bipolar or "affective psychosis"[110]—said about bipolar/manic patients that they were

> convinced of their superiority to their surroundings. . . . Towards others they are haughty, positive, irritable, impertinent, stubborn. . . . Unsteadiness and restlessness appear before everything. . . . With their surroundings the patients often live in constant feud.[111]

F.K. Goodwin and K.R. Jamison write about Kraepelin's definition of bipolar in their book *Manic-Depressive Illness: Bipolar Disorders and Recurrent Depression* that the underlying problem in

---

[107] Ibid., 819.

[108] Ibid., 822.

[109] R. Knowles, S. McCarthy-Jones, and G. Rowse, "Grandiose Delusions: A Review and Theoretical Integration of Cognitive and Affective Perspectives," *Clinical Psychology Review* 4 (June 31, 2011): 684-96.

[110] Berger, *Necessity for Faith and Authority*, 63-71.

[111] Emil Kraepelin, *Manic Depressive Insanity and Paranoia (Dementia Praecox and Paraphrenia)*, translated by Mary Barclay (Edinburgh: E. and S. Livingstone, 1921), 126-28.

a person diagnosed as bipolar is the person's temperament (their nature or character) as expressed in his or her thinking and behavior:

> In manic temperament, Kraepelin went on to say, the patients' "understanding of life and the world remains superficial"; their "train of thought is desultory, incoherent, aimless"; and their mood is "permanently exalted, careless, confident."[112]

If a person's nature is to be self-reliant and to seemingly wander aimlessly through life attempting to assuage all sorrow and hopelessness, then that individual will most likely be judged as a manic. The modern version of Kraepelin's definition of madness found in the *DSM-5* still describes one of the key characteristics of manic episodes: "Inflated self-esteem is typically present, ranging from uncritical self-confidence to marked grandiosity, and may reach delusional proportions."[113] But in truth, all self-esteem that is inflated is delusional.

When personality is characterized by thoughts of superiority, false fixed beliefs, and subsequent impairing behavior, the APA has decided this expression of madness to be either a "personality disorder,"[114] "schizophrenia" or some "other psychotic disorder" with "grandiose delusions,"[115] or "bipolar" with psychotic episodes during mania (once called "affective psychosis").[116] Despite the various nomenclatures assigned to describe alleged types of madness, pride—a false and exulted opinion of one's self—remains a major component of the modern secular constructs of madness.

Once again, it is observed that there is a clear agreement between the APA and Scripture that a false grandiose opinion of

---

112 F.K. Goodwin and K.R. Jamison, *Manic-Depressive Illness: Bipolar Disorders and Recurrent Depression* (Oxford: Oxford University Press, 1990), 82-83.

113 APA, *DSM-5*, 128.

114 Ibid., 817.

115 Ibid., 87.

116 Ibid., 822.

one's self is regularly associated with madness. Also apparent in both perspectives is that a haughty spirit leads to impairment and ultimately to destruction.

CONCLUSION

Both the biblical and psychiatric definitions recognize that the core of madness is false fixed beliefs. Yet, despite faith and deception being the true substance of insanity, explanatory theories, approaches, and suggested remedies for madness have largely shifted from a spiritual approach to a material perspective in many people's minds.

What Scripture and psychiatric theory can also agree on is that a person's false beliefs are most often revealed in one of three ways: (1) by rejecting truth that is inconvenient or goes against one's established worldview, (2) by enduring traumatic, unbearable, or difficult life experiences that cannot be explained away or resolved by a person's worldview or faith, (3) and by naturally being incapable of accepting spiritual truth by faith which alone can resolve or remedy human mindsets such as guilt, pride, deception, anxiety, hopelessness, and other mental struggles that characterize our spiritual blindness/false faith/depravity. Whether from the biblical perspective or the modern secular view—the bookends of history, madness is defined consistently as fixed faith in falsehood.

To deny the uniform and historical evidence across opposing worldviews and different cultures while continuing to claim that madness cannot be objectively defined is to embrace falsehood despite clear evidence. And yet today, many still believe that madness or mental illness is an abstract concept that has changed over time. This delusion highlights one major component in the sustained insanity of the theory of madness.

CHAPTER 3

UNDERSTANDING MODERN MADNESS

"Man's major foe is deep within him. But the enemy is no longer the same. Formerly it was ignorance; today it is falsehood."[117]
Jean-Francois Revel, philosopher

"The dilution of the concept of mental illness is to such a degree that it is no longer meaningful."[118]
Hagop Akiskal, psychiatrist

Though the previous chapter compared the biblical views with modern secular positions, it is beneficial for better understanding to examine the psychiatric perspective of mental illness more carefully. It is here—on the later end of history—that we find the most novel definition of madness produced by the American Psychiatric Association (APA) and published in the "psychiatric bible,"[119] the *Diagnostic and Statistical Manual 5th edition* (*DSM-5*). Gary Greenberg remarks on the significance of the *DSM*,

---

[117] Jean-Francois Revel, *The Flight from Truth* (New York: Random House, 1991), 18.

[118] Hagop S. Akiskal and William T. McKinney, Jr., "Psychiatry and Pseudopsychiatry," *Archives of General Psychiatry* 28 (1973): 372.

[119] Lieberman, *Shrinks*, 87-88.

> The book is the basis of psychiatrists' authority to pronounce upon our mental health, to command health care dollars from insurance companies for treatment and from government agencies for research. It is as important to psychiatrists as the Constitution is to the US government or the Bible is to Christians. Outside the profession, too, the *DSM* rules, serving as the authoritative text for psychologists, social workers, and other mental health workers; it is invoked by lawyers in arguing over the culpability of criminal defendants and by parents seeking school services for their children.[120]

The *DSM-5* merely represents the latest secular attempt to explain the age-old problem of human madness.

While the philosophical vantage points of the *DSM-5* and the Bible are in opposition, their foundational definitions of madness are surprisingly the same. Where these two positions differ greatly is in their theories and explanations of what causes and remedies madness. In large part, the many secular theories over the last two centuries have hidden the true definition of insanity. Still, unbelief/false faith/delusions/rejection of reality remain the core of madness, unchanged throughout history.

THE PSYCHIATRIC TERMS

What has also changed across time and cultures and added to the confusion and imprecision of madness are names used to describe it. In the last two centuries, psychiatric theorists across the globe have assigned countless new terms to describe their own theories of false beliefs and corresponding behavior. *Lunacy,*[121] *insanity, neurosis, hysteria, craziness, mental illness, mental disorder, delusional thinking, unhealthy thinking, mania, splitting, schizophrenia, dissociation, abnormality, psychosis, intoxication, doubling,* and *psychic numbing* are some of the more well-known terms used in the last two centuries to reflect one's disconnect from truth, denial of reality, and embrace of false

---

120 Greenberg, "Battle to Define Mental Illness."

121 "'Lunacy' originally referred to the [false] belief that intermittent phases of mental derangement were causally related to phases of the moon" (Pietikäinen, *Madness*, 7).

belief. With the many terms used to describe madness, there are equal numbers of opinions about how each of these terms should be defined and how madness/psychosis/mental illness should be divided (or not) and categorized.

Prior to the APA's creation of the *DSM-5*, psychiatrists, psychologists, and other physicians alike commonly created their own systems of evaluating behavior and determining what they considered to be madness. Lieberman remarks,

> Despite the existence of the standard, in the early twentieth century there was nothing approaching consensus on the basic categories of mental illness.[122]

The *DSM* would not only suggest a standard, albeit in the form of a constantly changing and imprecise manual, but it would also provide a system of categorizing different types of madness and a different way of explaining it.

In fact, the term *madness* became taboo, since it undermined psychiatry's new paradigm and challenged psychiatrists' self-asserted control over the concept of insanity. Historian Andrew Scull notes,

> Madness is no longer an acceptable term to use in polite company. For psychiatrists, its use is a provocation, an implicit rejection of their claims to expertise in the diagnosis and treatment of mental disorders, and symptomatic of a willful refusal to accept the findings of modern medical science.[123]

The terms may have changed, but the core elements remain the same. In the place of *madness*, the term *mental illness* now reigns.

Not only did the term change, several other important things did too. For one, madness was historically a singular condition of the soul, whereas the concept of mental illness divided madness into a plurality; it suggested different types of madness

---

[122] Ibid., 91.

[123] Scull, *Madness*, 1.

rather than the historical unitary definition.[124] Likewise, madness had become a medical issue, or rather, the medical community had framed madness in such a way (focusing on medical theories of etiologies and remedies and popularizing the term *mental illness*) that it could control the concept and make psychiatry relevant. The *American Psychiatric Publishing Textbook of Forensic Psychiatry* states,

> The process by which medicine came to dominate discourse concerning mental illness has engendered debate and controversy among historians and sociologists of science and medicine (Scull 1981a). The controversies revolve around the validity of different perspectives of historiography. Internal histories of medicines, often written by medical practitioners, tend to portray medical history as the progressive advancement of objective knowledge and humanitarian benefits, generally without reference to external forces. Critics of this approach point out that *conceptualizations of diseases and treatments unquestionably demonstrate the imprint of social and cultural forces*, and failure to consider these forces results in an incomplete and biased perception of historical events [emphasis added].[125]

Understanding historical madness offers a foundational definition of mental illness. Similarly, Ethan Watters comments,

> We can become psychologically unhinged for many reasons that are common to all, like personal traumas, social upheavals or biochemical imbalances in our brains. Modern science has begun to reveal these causes. *Whatever the trigger, however, the ill individual and those around him invariably rely on cultural beliefs and stories to understand what is happening*. . . . In the end, what cross-cultural psychiatrists and anthropologists have to tell us is that all mental illness, including depression, P.T.S.D. and even schizophrenia, can be every bit as influenced by cultural beliefs and expectations today as hysterical-leg paralysis or the vapors or zar [an idea similar to demonic possession] or any other mental illness ever experienced in the history of human madness. This does not mean that these illnesses and the pain associated with them are not real, or that sufferers deliberately shape

---

124 "'Unitary psychosis' is the collective name for a set of disparate doctrines whose common denominator is the view that there is only one form of psychosis and that its diverse clinical presentations can be explained in terms of endogenous and exogenous factors" (G.E. Berrios and D. Beer, "The Notion of Unitary Psychosis: A Conceptual History," *History of Psychiatry* 5, no. 17 [March 1, 1994]: 13–14.

125 Robert Simon and Liza Gold, eds., *American Psychiatric Publishing Textbook of Forensic Psychiatry* (Washington, D.C.: American Psychiatric Publishing, 2010), 5.

> their symptoms to fit a certain cultural niche. *It means that a mental illness is an illness of the mind and cannot be understood without understanding the ideas, habits and predispositions – the idiosyncratic cultural trappings – of the mind that is its host.* [emphases added][126]

Madness has remained the same throughout history, but a new philosophical filter of materialism has been imposed upon false fixed beliefs and the mind that conceives them. This new construct attempts to medicalize all false beliefs and mental fragility into disease entities.

Along with the modern psychiatric term *mental illness* is the idea of *psychosis*, psychiatry's preferred term to explain historic madness.[127] More specifically, *psychosis* is the primary word that defines and explains today's "major disorders" or the most "serious mental illnesses."[128] The term *psychosis* is derived from the Greek words *psyche* (soul) and *osis* (condition) – meaning a "condition of the soul."[129] Psychosis, then, is a new attempt to explain the old problem of false fixed beliefs – a deceived condition of the soul that is impairing and destructive.

While the APA insists that mental illness cannot be objectively defined, it offers a precise definition of psychosis in the *DSM-5*. Clinicians use this agreed upon definition of psychosis as a diagnostic standard to identify madness:

---

126 Ethan Watters, "The Americanization of Mental Illness," *New York Times*, January 8, 2010, MM40. Also available from http://www.nytimes.com/2010/01/10/magazine/10psyche-t.html.

127 The term *psychosis* was introduced by Ernst von Feuchtersleben as a replacement for the word *madness*. M. Dominic Beer, "Psychosis: From Mental Disorder to Disease Concept," *History of Psychiatry* 6, no. 22 (June 1, 1995): 177-200.

128 "This uncertainty at the core of psychiatry creates a slippery diagnostic slope. Severe illnesses such as schizophrenia and major depression tend to present relatively clear signs (delusions, hallucinations, catatonia, psychomotor problems). But milder disorders of mood and anxiety can share symptoms with ordinary reactions to life events" (Pettus, "Psychiatry by Prescription").

129 The suffix *-osis* is used to describe many valid medical conditions (e.g., chlorosis, neurofibromatosis, tuberculosis, leukocytosis etc.), and it is also used to express conditions in non-medicinal applications (e.g., metamorphosis means a change in physical condition).

"Features characterized by delusions, hallucinations, and formal thought disorder."[130] The APA also defines these "characteristics" of psychosis with clarity. A delusion, for example, is

> a *false belief based* on *incorrect inference* about external reality that is firmly held despite what almost everyone else *believes* and despite what constitutes incontrovertible and obvious proof or evidence to the contrary [emphasis added]."[131]

The term *delusion* is derived from Latin and means "a deceiving."[132] At their very core, delusions are false beliefs which deny or incorrectly surmise reality. Likewise, the word *hallucination* is objectively defined as

> a *perception-like experience* with the clarity and impact of a *true perception* but without the *external stimulation* of the relevant sensory organ. . . . One hallucinating person may recognize the *false sensory experience*, whereas another may be convinced that the experience is grounded in *reality* [emphases added].[133]

In other words, hallucinations are false perceptions about physical stimuli that do not exist; they are sensations that are falsely believed to be real. The difference between delusions and hallucinations, then, is the content of the false beliefs. False beliefs that are not related to the senses and are considered abstract ideas are classified as delusions, whereas false beliefs that relate to sensory experiences (beliefs about the physical world related to the senses) are designated as hallucinations.

The last major criterion for determining psychosis is "formal thought disorder," which is another way to say disorderly or poor thinking. The only way to recognize thought disorder is from evaluating a person's words or forms of communication. Richard Bentall comments,

---

130 APA, *DSM-5*, 827.

131 Ibid., 819.

132 https://www.etymonline.com/word/delusion.

133 APA, *DSM-5*, 822.

> The ability to speak has a profound effect on all other aspects of the human mind, and therefore must be considered when we attempt to understand the role of cognition in psychosis. When thinking about the function language plays in human life, it is only natural to regard it as a means by which information is passed from one individual to another.[134]

Thus, this criterion is regularly referred to as "word salad," since it simply represents odd, unusual, or jumbled speech that reflects a person's thoughts:

> Disorganized thinking is typically inferred from the individual's speech. The individual may switch from one topic to another . . . . Rarely, speech may be so severely disorganized that it is nearly incomprehensible and resembles receptive aphasia in its linguistic disorganization (incoherence or "word salad").[135]

Delusions, hallucinations, and formal thought disorders—the true substance of psychiatry's modern concept of psychosis/madness—are all foundationally falsehoods that are manifested in words and behavior (including catatonic behavior and negative symptoms[136]). Psychiatrist Emil Kraepelin, who invented the constructs of what are today called *schizophrenia* and *bipolar disorders,* described this condition of the soul in the early 1900s:

> Words are whispered inside him. The devil speaks out of the heart of the patient; he swears in him; the patient hears him "inwardly, not with his ears." "An inward voice from the heart says filthy things about God," said a female patient. Another heard "voices coming from within, which lament." "There is talking in my head along with my thoughts," declared a third. The voices generally stand in the most intimate relation to the reaming content of consciousness. The patients declare that they are questioned; their thoughts are repeated loud out

---

134 Bentall, *Madness Explained,* 295.

135 APA, *DSM-5,* 88.

136 The APA lists *Catatonic Behavior* ("ranging from childlike 'silliness' to unpredictable agitation") and *Negative Symptoms* (emotional distress) as two other criteria for schizophrenia (APA, *DSM-5,* 88). These behaviors are said to be a disconnect from one's environment or reality (ibid.), and they are best understood as effects of one's false thinking as well as many times the effects of antipsychotic drugs (e.g., tardive dyskinesia).

> after two or three minutes. Others carry on conversations with their voices.[137]

The common underlying factor in delusions, hallucinations, and thought disorder is invisible false beliefs and perceptions which are revealed in various observable behaviors. Dr. Reznek spells out the five recognized aspects of delusions by psychiatrists:

> All definitions contain a number of ingredients—that a delusion is a belief, that it is held firmly against evidence to the contrary, that it is false, and that it is out of keeping with cultural beliefs. According to standard psychiatric thinking, then, something is a delusion if and only if: (1) it is a belief (Belief Axiom); (2) it is held with conviction (Conviction Axiom); (3) it is held in the face of obvious evidence to the contrary (Incorrigibility Axiom); it is false (Reality Axiom); and (5) it is out of keeping with the person's community (Community Axiom).[138]

Despite the change in nomenclature (from madness to mental illness or psychosis) and attempts to attribute madness to biological etiologies, the core of madness is unchanged. False fixed beliefs made manifest in one's words and behavior objectively defines madness.

THE PSYCHIATRIC PARADIGM

Throughout most of history, people have regarded madness as a singular problem handled by religious and community leaders.[139] In the early 1800s, however, that position would begin to change due in large part to psychiatrists who were designated to watch over the insane and guard society from them. Given this new control, psychiatrists began to theorize about insanity, and eventually through their medical perspective, they changed the way madness was explained and treated.

It is Karl Kahbaum whom some historians credit with first suggesting a plurality of madness. While he did not specifically

---

137 Kraepelin, *Manic Depressive Insanity and Paranoia*, 11.

138 Reznek, *Delusions and Madness of the Masses*, preface xvii.

139 Shorter, *A History of Psychiatry*, 104.

define madness as various diseases per se, Kahbaum's theory opened the door for an entirely new definition of madness – one that perceived insanity as a plurality and as "distinctive diseases.[140] Psychiatrists would soon begin their attempt to "cut nature at the joints."[141]

While Kahbaum is credited with conceptualizing a plurality of madness, it is Emil Kraepelin,[142] a German psychiatrist and student of Wilhelm Wundt, who made famous the notion that madness should be categorized into various types and viewed as separate disease entities.[143] Thus, most every historian considers Kraepelin to be the father of modern psychiatry and the creator of the current construct of mental illness.[144] He is also credited with being one of the first to speculate that false fixed beliefs might have discoverable physical causes (pathology) which, in Kraepelin's mind, could explain the different observable behavior: "One of the most important achievements of Emil Kraepelin was the connection of pathogenesis [how disease originates] and manifestation of psychiatric disorders."[145] Two hundred years later and despite major scientific advancements in medicine, however, Kraepelin's proposed theory of

---

140 Historian Ed Shorter notes that it was Karl Kahlbaum who produced the "first clinical description of schizophrenia with the claim that it represented a distinctive disease." Kahlbaum's distinctions were more of onset and degrees and not actually diseases apart from the idea of psychosis (e.g., child onset psychosis was called "hebephrenia") (Shorter, *A History of Psychiatry*, 104).

141 Ibid., 106.

142 Ibid., 69.

143 "The dichotomic concept of psychosis is the best-known part of Kraepelin's psychiatric work," (Andreas Ebert and Karl-Jürgen Bär, "Emil Kraepelin: A Pioneer of Scientific Understanding of Psychiatry and Psychopharmacology," *Indian Journal of Psychiatry* 52, no. 2 [2010]: 191–92).

144 For further study on Emil Kraepelin, see Berger, *Necessity for Faith and Authority*, 63-71.

145 Ebert and Bär, "Emil Kraepelin," 191–92.

pathogenesis to explain false fixed beliefs still lacks validating empirical evidence.[146]

Kraepelin's theory of madness revolutionized psychiatric ideology and still controls the vast majority of psychiatric thinking today: "His influence over the world's conception and diagnosis of mental illness would eventually rival—and then surpass—that of Sigmund Freud."[147] Kraepelin was not the first to suggest that there were different types of mental illnesses, but his published classification system placed him firmly in the historical spotlight.

Kraepelin first divided madness into two large groups: what is now called schizophrenia and what is now thought to be unipolar and bipolar depression. The historian Ed Shorter remarks,

> Thus by 1899, Kraepelin had elevated the two greater nonorganic [the invisible] ("functional") psychoses—manic-depressive illness and schizophrenia—to the top of the pyramid, where they remain in only slightly modified form to this day as the object of endeavor of serious psychiatry.[148]

In seeming to have divided madness into separate diseases, Kraepelin enabled psychiatry to be viewed, not as social work or a custodial service, but as a valid medical profession that

---

[146] "As scientific understanding of the brain advances, the APA has found itself caught between paradigms, forced to revise a manual that everyone agrees needs to be fixed but with no obvious way forward. [Darrel] Regier [director of research and vice-chair of the *DSM-5* task force] says he's hopeful that "full understanding of the underlying pathophysiology of mental disorders" will someday establish an "absolute threshold between normality and psychopathology." Realistically, though, a new manual based entirely on neuroscience—with biomarkers for every diagnosis, grave or mild—seems decades away, and perhaps impossible to achieve at all. To account for mental suffering entirely through neuroscience is probably tantamount to explaining the brain in *toto,* a task to which our scientific tools may never be matched. As [Allen] Frances points out, a complete elucidation of the complexities of the brain has so far proven to be an "ever-receding target" (Greenberg, "Battle to Define Mental Illness").

[147] Lieberman, *Shrinks,* 92.

[148] Shorter, *A History of Psychiatry,* 107.

oversaw a variety of newly discovered diseases. The division of madness into seemingly separate concepts along with the acceptance of materialism in much of society enabled psychiatry's acceptance as a legitimate medical field:

> In giving a careful account of dementia praecox, or schizophrenia, as a distinct disease, Kraepelin had handed psychiatry its most powerful term of the twentieth century.[149]

Kraepelin's classifications of mindsets and behavior once posited as madness not only empowered psychiatry, it would also popularize the belief that there existed different types of madness. Such a reality is precisely why former president of the Royal College of Psychiatrists R.E. Kendell once said,

> If any man were bold enough to write a history of psychiatric classifications, he would find when he had completed his task that in the process he had written a history of psychiatry as well.[150]

Though Kraepelin seemingly divided madness into different types, he actually continued to view them as various manifestations of a unitary madness. In his mind, his classifications represented not different diseases—as is suggested today, but different corresponding effects born out of different delusions. In fact, Kraepelin wrote in the sixth edition of his book *Psychiatry*, "In the course of the years I have become more and more convinced that all [psychiatric labels] are really just *manifestations of a single disease process* [emphasis added]."[151] He also asserted about his suggested groups of mental illness,

> Experienced observers will not fail to notice that the validity of the definitions of specific groups presented here can in no way claim to be unanimously accepted. Consequently, they are of no further scientific value; but they might—due to their emphasis on certain practically

---

[149] Ibid., 106.

[150] R. E. Kendell, *The Role of Diagnosis in Psychiatry* (Oxford: Blackwell, 1975), 176.

[151] Emil Kraepelin, *Psychiatrie*, 6th ed. (Leipzig: Barth, 1899), 359.

> important fundamentals—help give students an overview of the diversity of closely related clinical cases.[152]

However one might attempt to rewrite history, Kraepelin's classification, which the current *DSM-5* follows, once described insanity as manifestations of a singular madness and not different types as is believed today. In his own words, Kraepelin acknowledged that his attempt to divide madness into groups was not objective and had "no further scientific value."

Many psychiatrists and other clinicians are arriving at the realization that what is presented as historical fact about Kraepelin is often inaccurate and imposed upon the figure by "neo-Kraepelinians" (those who dogmatically believe his theory and control the mental health system today). Psychologist E.J. Engsrom and psychiatrist K.S. Kendler, for example, comment in the abstract of their article, "Emil Kraepelin: Icon and Reality," published in the *American Journal of Psychiatry*:

> In the last third of the 20th century, the German psychiatrist Emil Kraepelin (1856-1926) became an icon of postpsychoanalytic medical-model psychiatry in the United States. His name became synonymous with a proto-biological, antipsychological, brain-based, and hard-nosed nosologic approach to psychiatry. This article argues that this contemporary image of Kraepelin fails to appreciate the historical contexts in which he worked and misrepresents his own understanding of his clinical practice and research. A careful rereading and contextualization of his inaugural lecture on becoming chair of psychiatry at the University of Tartu (known at the time as the University of Dorpat) in 1886 and of the numerous editions of his famous textbook reveals that Kraepelin was, compared with our current view of him, 1) far more psychologically inclined and stimulated by the exciting early developments of scientific psychology, 2) considerably less brain-centric, and 3) nosologically more skeptical and less doctrinaire. Instead of a quest for a single "true" diagnostic system, his nosological agenda was expressly pragmatic and tentative: he sought to sharpen boundaries for didactic reasons and to develop diagnoses that served critical clinical needs, such as the prediction of illness course. The historical Kraepelin, who struggled with how to interrelate brain and mind-based approaches to psychiatric illness, and who appreciated the strengths and limitations of his clinically based nosology, still has quite a bit to teach

---

[152] Ibid., 212.

modern psychiatry and can be a more generative forefather than the icon created by the neo-Kraepelinians.[153]

Ironically, what the psychiatrists who wrote this journal entry point out is that neo-Kraepelinian psychiatrists are often delusional about the history and theoretical positions of their forefather. Kraepelin's sordid past and some of his historical theories do not fit the narrative for today's biological model of madness; still, these are facts which must be considered.

In his later years of life, Kraepelin vacillated between believing that madness should be viewed as many diseases (mental illnesses) and holding that there existed only a unitary madness. On the one hand, he realized that madness was a singular problem; while on the other hand, he hoped to make madness a scientific and medical endeavor in order to advance his projected target for psychiatry. The only way to transform madness into a medical issue and make psychiatry a legitimate medical field, he believed, was to prove not only that madness was biologically caused, but also that it was comprised of multiple diseases.

In Kraepelin's original subjective construct of insanity, he created two main groups (later he added the concept of paranoia to make three[154]): *dementia praecox* (psychosis or today called schizophrenic disorders) and *affective psychosis* (manic-depressive insanity or known today as bipolar disorders). While behaviors slightly varied, both categories shared the same underlying problem of deception or disconnection from reality. Dr. Lieberman notes that

> Kraepelin's classification scheme was immediately marked by controversy because dementia praecox and manic-depressive illness had usually been considered manifestation of the same underlying disorder, though Kraepelin justified the distinction by pointing out that

---

153 E.J. Engstrom and K.S. Kendler, "Emil Kraepelin: Icon and Reality," *American Journal of Psychiatry* 172, no. 12 (December 1, 2015): 1190-96, https://doi.org/10.1176/appi.ajp.2015.15050665.

154 Lieberman, *Shrinks*, 94.

> manic-depressive illness was episodic rather than continuous, like dementia praecox.[155]

This common characteristic is now referred to as *psychosis* or *mania* and, as pointed out, amounts to false fixed beliefs. Both Kraepelinian constructs (schizophrenia and bipolar), though, describe someone who is not willing to accept reality and thus is delusional. The distinction is in the frequency of deception, in the content of the false beliefs, and in how it manifests in different behavior (though the beliefs and behaviors are often the same). Some theorists argue that emotional states constitute a differential between the two alleged disorders,[156] but that argument has been dismissed. Clinical psychologist Richard Bentall, for instance, argues that all forms of psychosis (e.g., schizophrenia and bipolar) include one's emotions; since emotions are simply a way to describe how thoughts manifest into behavior:

> It is in fact quite difficult to distinguish between emotions and other feelings such as pain or hunger, or other types of mental contents such as attitudes and beliefs. Textbooks of psychology routinely observe that emotions have affective (feeling), cognitive (thoughts and beliefs), and behavioral components, which should alert us to the possibility that the ordinary language word 'emotion' does not refer to a single process.[157]

What are called emotions (e.g., anger, sadness, fear etc.) are never separate from mindsets/beliefs and are most often observed in behavior. As Bentall notes, if beliefs are false, so too will be one's emotions and behavior. It is no wonder, then, that both those who are diagnosed as being bipolar and those who are diagnosed as being schizophrenic struggle with depression and maladaptive moods.[158]

---

155 Ibid., 94.

156 Watters and Ofshe, *Therapy's Delusions*, 22.

157 Bentall, *Madness Explained*, 207.

158 Ibid., 205-10.

In truth, Kraepelin understood that the mindsets and behaviors which allegedly differentiate bipolar disorder from schizophrenia were not enough to dogmatically and categorically divide madness. According to historian Ed Shorter,

> In 1920 Kraepelin softened slightly the watertight division between affective and nonaffective psychoses by admitting that the prognosis could not always be made on the basis of the presenting symptoms [beliefs and behaviors].[159]

Not surprising, in his eighth edition of *Psychiatry (1913)*, Kraepelin abandoned many proposed disorders/categories of madness that he had previously published as fact.[160] His attempt to divide madness had left him recognizing different manifestations of madness and not various types. Could it be that mental illness is simply one human problem that manifests in different ways rather than different diseases?

But as Kraepelin himself noted, different behavior alone is not enough to turn madness into a plural concept.[161] The other important factor, Kraepelin believed, was frequency and duration of the symptoms across a person's life: "Kraepelin decided to organize illnesses not just by symptoms alone but also according to the course of each illness."[162] This new thinking introduced a time or duration qualifier as a diagnostic tool to differentiate between alleged disorders and normalcy as well as a diagnostic system to categorize mindsets, behavior, and frequency.

Near the end of his life, Kraepelin seems to have believed that the different manifestations of false beliefs amounted to different diseases. Today's psychiatric construct of mental illness contained in the *DSM-5* and other secular classification

---

159 Shorter, *A History of Psychiatry*, 356.

160 Ibid., 356.

161 Emil Kraepelin, "Die Erscheinungsformen des Irreseins," *Zeitschrift fur die gesamte Neurologie und Psychiatrie*, 62 (1920), 27.

162 Lieberman, *Shrinks*, 93.

systems[163] follows Kraepelin's belief,[164] though the APA does acknowledge that the lines of demarcation between alleged disorders are fluid:

> In *DSM-5*, we recognize that the current diagnostic criteria for any single disorder will not necessarily identify a homogeneous group of patients who can be characterized reliably with all of these validators. Available evidence shows that these validators cross existing diagnostic boundaries but tend to congregate more frequently within and across adjacent *DSM-5* chapter groups. Until incontrovertible etiological or pathophysiological mechanisms are identified to fully validate specific disorder or disorder spectra, the most important standard for the *DSM-5* disorder criteria will be their clinical utility for the assessment of clinical course and treatment response of individuals grouped by a given set of diagnostic criteria.[165]

The various disorders in the *DSM-5* are not valid or reliable disease entities with pathophysiological mechanisms or biological markers; they are merely speculative beliefs based on Kraepelin's original theory.

Despite the acceptance and popularity of Kraepelin's asserted theory today, the underlying problem of false fixed beliefs remains the premier mark of madness. Kraepelin had not discovered types of madness or new diseases; rather, he had simply labeled and categorized different false fixed beliefs by their content, duration, and common manifestations. Today, the debate over whether madness is unitary or a plurality remains an often-heated discussion and sub-types continue to expand as duration and slightly different manifestations are further divided.

---

163 The *International Classification of Diseases* (*ICD*) is owned by the World Health Organization and could someday replace the *DSM* as the premier secular mental health classification system. There is a growing movement—especially among psychologists—to make the *ICD* the standard of mental illness diagnosis (APA, "*ICD* vs. *DSM*," *Monitor on Psychology* 40, no. 9 [Oct 2009]: 63).

164 "Both the International Classification of Diseases (WHO) as well as APA's *DSM*-Classification still rely on Kraepelin's concept" (Ebert and Bär, "Emil Kraepelin," 191–192).

165 APA, *DSM-5*, 20.

THE PSYCHIATRIC DISORDERS

Though the American Psychiatric Association utilizes the Kraepelinian construct of mental illness and the concept of psychosis to facilitate its explanation of so-called severe madness, it has also created numerous constructs to describe other common false fixed beliefs. Instead of the original two diseases that Kraepelin first proposed, today's construct of mental illness now contains over 400 separate mental illnesses. If Kraepelin split madness at its joints, the APA has split the cells. It has done so by suggesting numerous sub-types for each suggested mental disorder contained in the *DSM-5*. In the APA's view, such continued division represents medical and scientific advancement.

The vast majority of psychiatric constructs of mental illness, though, simply describe specific false beliefs or normal human frailty/weakness; they reveal the mindset of someone who is deceived and typically distressed at some level. The key differentials between these psychiatric constructs of mental illness in the *DSM-5* are the content, frequency, and observable manifested behavior of the false beliefs. If we remove valid physical illnesses (e.g., dementia, Fetal Alcohol Syndrome, Fragile X Syndrome, Alzheimer's, and autism spectrum disorder; what society once referred to as "idiocy") from the *DSM-5* and examine the various constructs of mental illness more carefully, we discover that madness remains a singular idea with various manifestations.

Bipolar/Schizophrenia Spectrum/DID Disorders

The central component that the constructs of bipolar, schizophrenia, and dissociative identity disorder (DID) share is false fixed beliefs and perceptions. In fact, Emil Kraepelin first described the characteristics of "manic-depressive insanity" (one of the original names assigned to what is now called bipolar disorder) as virtually mirroring today's psychiatric descriptions of DID and schizophrenia:

> The patient hears a murmuring and a whispering, a roaring, the crackling of hell; he hears someone coming up the steps, going to the "larder," "the devil carrying on in the walls," "death gnashing his teeth in the wall, noises as if a corpse were being thrown out at the window," an uproar in the stove as if a man wanted to get into it. There are noises in his head. It sounds like tolling of bells and the murmur of the ocean, like cries for help, shooting, the death rattle and "groaning, screaming and howling, weeping, entreating and lamenting, clamoring and cursing." "In all the noises there is something, "said a patient in very significant tones. Spirits buzz about each other; others snarl something which has some connection with the patient. Occasionally the illusions are related to definite impressions. The birds call out the name of the patient; they whistle, "Come, Emily." The clock says, "You dog, you're the devil, a swine." The rhythmic vascular murmur in the ear becomes a reproach, "bad, bad," or "whore, whore," which then is ascribed to the devil. . . . At night disguised figures come into the room. The patient sees an open grave, his dead wife, the apostle Paul with good angels, the Saviour on the cross, the Virgin Mary, Jesus with roses, the living God, the devil, He sees corpses, skeletons, sad spirits, monsters, the heads of his children on the wall, fiery things which signify his sins.[166]

Kraepelin later wrote,

> In Manic-Depressive Insanity [there is] the devil's laugh, the weeping of the dead mother, the screaming of children, the song of angels. The content of the hallucinations of hearing is usually unpleasant and alarming. All possible sins are brought before the patient as if he were a criminal; he is enticed to suicide. . . . "Do something [bad] to yourself," "hang yourself," "If he would only hang himself, otherwise we must keep him for ten years yet."[167]

Thus the first psychiatric descriptions of alleged bipolar disorder—penned by the father of today's psychiatric paradigm of mental illness—identified false fixed beliefs or deception to be the true nature of madness.

The APA still recognizes false fixed beliefs about one's self to be the genuine problem described in the manic state of the construct of bipolar disorder. It describes mania as "inflated self-esteem or grandiosity."[168] Later the APA asserts in the *DSM-5*:

---

166 Kraepelin, *Manic Depressive Insanity and Paranoia,* 9.

167 Ibid.

168 APA, *DSM-5*, 124.

> Inflated self-esteem is typically present, ranging from uncritical self-confidence to marked grandiosity, and may reach delusional proportions (Criterion B1). Despite lack of any particular experience or talent, the individual may embark on complex tasks such as writing a novel or seeking publicity for some impractical invention. *Grandiose delusions* (e.g., of having a special relationship to a famous person) *are common* [emphasis added].[169]

Though psychiatrists may not perceive some inflated self-esteem or uncritical self-confidence to be false beliefs, a person's false fixed belief about themselves is a delusion. The *DSM* also states of mania that people in a manic state disregard real risks and consequences in favor of fantasy and pleasure,[170] and they are deceived to the point that the *DSM* asserts that "during a manic episode, individuals often do not perceive that they are ill or in need of treatment and vehemently resist efforts to be treated."[171] "Mania" or "a manic episode" describes an "elevated mood" where the person "exaggerates" his/her feelings and thinking.[172] Some clinicians perceive that bipolar represents an often false bias toward perceiving people and their motives as either "overly positive" or "overly bad." [173] One author describes her own experience:

> Bipolar robs you of that which is you. It can take from you the very core of your being and replace it with something that is completely opposite of who and what you truly are. . . . Not only did bipolar rob me of my sanity, but it robbed me of my ability to see beyond the space it dictated me to look. I no longer could tell reality from fantasy, and I walked in a world no longer my own.[174]

---

169 Ibid., 128.

170 Ibid., 129.

171 Ibid.

172 Ibid., 824.

173 James Phelps, "Mood Bias: A Partial Explanation of Bipolar Disorder?" *Psychiatric Times Online* (January 16, 2018): http://www.psychiatrictimes.com/bipolar-disorder/mood-bias-partial-explanation-bipolardisorder/? GUID=31158D64-F01A-4DEA-AC1A-D3CE843FC9BC&rememberme=1&ts=18012018.

174 Alyssa Reyans, *Letters from a Bipolar Mother*, vol. 1 (Alyreyans Press, 2012), 8.

Kraepelin noted in the early 1900s that hallucinations are also sometimes experienced during manic states:

> Distinct pseudo-memories are not infrequently met with in the patients, especially in mania. . . . Occasionally they show in a pronounced manner a tendency to delusional tabulation, to descriptions of wonderful experiences out of the past, which the patients more or less seriously believe.[175]

In a similar manner, the APA describes *Dissociative Identity Disorder* (DID; what was once called *multi-personality disorder*) in the *DSM-5* this way:

> The defining feature of dissociative identity disorder is the presence of two or more distinct personality states or an experience of possession (Criterion A). . . . In many possession-form cases of dissociative identity disorder, and in a small proportion of non-possession-form cases, manifestations of alternate identities are highly overt.[176]

Whether it is actual demon possession or the utility of deception to deal with reality, deception and false fixed beliefs are at the core of DID. If delusions and hallucinations are characteristic of bipolar, schizophrenia, DID disorders, and all forms of alleged psychosis then what truly separates these constructs from one another? One thing is certain: falsehood is the root of each.

The father of modern psychiatric theory, Emil Kraepelin, admitted that differentiating between his originally suggested categories of insanity was only possible by observing behavior. Behavior, in conjunction with the content of false beliefs, is listed in the *DSM-5* as constituting the criteria for each of the suggested psychiatric disorders. But often even the behavior and mental content is the same between constructs. Kraepelin wrote toward the end of his life (1920),

> We shall have to get accustomed to the fact that our much-used clinical checklist does not permit us to differentiate reliably manic depressive insanity [now called bipolar disorder] from dementia praecox [now called schizophrenia] in all circumstances; and that there is an overlap

---

175 Kraepelin, *Manic Depressive Insanity and Paranoia*, 8.

176 Ibid., 292.

between the two, which depends on the fact that the clinical signs have arisen from certain antecedent conditions.[177]

Similarly, Eugen Bleuler did not believe that bipolar and schizophrenia were separate diseases.[178] It was, in fact, Bleuler who renamed Kraepelin's concept of *dementia praecox* as *schizophrenia* to better describe "the splitting of the mind" that seemingly occurs when people are psychotic.[179]

Many distinguished psychiatrists, such as R.E. Kendell (former president of the Royal College of Psychiatrists), realize that real boundaries between disorders may not actually exist:

> Few psychiatric disorders have yet been adequately validated and it is still an open issue whether there are genuine boundaries between the clinical syndromes recognized in contemporary classifications, or between these syndromes and normality.[180]

Others also recognize that schizophrenia and bipolar disorders are not actually separate forms of madness,

> The separation of affective disorders from schizophrenic psychosis as two distinct entities formed the basis for the understanding of psychiatric illnesses for more than a century. Over the last years both entities have been more and more regarded rather as a continuum than as two entirely distinct forms.[181]

One medical journal noted how acclaimed psychiatrists have historically seen madness as unitary:

> As recently as 1963 one of America's most distinguished psychiatrists of today, Karl Menninger, put forward virtually the same hypothesis

---

177 Kraepelin, "Clinical Manifestations of Mental Illness," 499-529.

178 Goodwin and Jamison, *Manic-Depressive Illness*, 8, 89-112.

179 Berger, *Necessity for Dependence*, 66-69.

180 R.E. Kendell, "Clinical Validity," *Psychological Medicine* (1) (February 19, 1989), 45.

181 Ebert and Bär, "Emil Kraepelin," 191.

["unitary psychosis"] and insisted the schizophrenia was merely a convenient term for the more severe forms of mental illness.[182]

Clinical psychologist Richard Bentall also comments that these alleged disorders are too alike to dogmatically claim them as separate disorders,

> The most likely explanation for the strong associations observed between schizophrenia, depression, and mania is that these diagnoses do not describe separate disorders.[183]

Even the APA itself admits in the *DSM-5* that "we have come to recognize that the boundaries between disorders are more porous than originally perceived."[184] This pre-Kraepelin way of thinking is framed as a new theory by the APA and referred to in the *DSM-5* as the "dimensional approach":[185]

> The results of numerous studies of comorbidity and disease transmission in families, including twin studies and molecular genetic studies, make strong arguments for what many astute clinicians have long observed: *the boundaries between many disorder "categories" are more fluid over the life course than DSM-IV recognized, and many symptoms assigned to a single disorder may occur, at varying levels of severity, in many other disorders.* These findings mean that the *DSM*, like other medical disease classifications, should accommodate ways to introduce *dimensional approaches* to mental disorders, including dimensions that cut across current categories [emphasis added].[186]

Essentially, the APA admits in their suggested "dimensional approach" that how Kraepelin and most psychiatrists thereafter have attempted to divide madness is not as credible and reliable as suggested all these years. But promoting the idea of madness as a plurality all these years was vital to reframe deceit as a disease entity (mental illness). The return to what was "long

---

182 Rollin, Henry R. "The Role of Diagnosis in Psychiatry." *British Medical Journal* 1.6005 (1976): 348.

183 Bentall, *Madness Explained*, 71.

184 APA, *DSM-5*, 6.

185 Ibid., 5.

186 Ibid.

observed" — a disguised unitary approach now referred to as the "dimensional approach" — reveals that the true underlying nature of madness/mental illness is singular.

The construct of "schizoaffective disorder" (the combination of schizophrenia and bipolar disorders) provides a great illustration of the APA's uncertainty about the theoretical boundaries of their constructs. The APA suggests that the key diagnostic feature of the disorder is "an uninterrupted period of illness during which there is a major mood episode (major depressive or manic) concurrent with Criterion A of schizophrenia."[187] But if the psychiatric constructs of schizophrenia and bipolar (and unipolar depression) are understood to represent different delusions rather than different diseases, the construct of schizoaffective disorder becomes an unnecessary theory and reveals that it is not a valid disease. Such a reality may explain why the APA also admits in the *DSM-5* that "there is a growing evidence that schizoaffective disorder is not a distinct nosological category."[188] Though it remains an alleged disease in the current *DSM*, schizoaffective disorder will most likely be removed from future editions.

While many psychiatrists continue to claim that madness is a plural concept, there is much evidence to the contrary. Most notable is the fact that false fixed beliefs characterize all major forms of modern madness. It makes little sense, then, apart from attempting to sustain a medical theory of madness to separate deceptive mindsets by their content and declare them to be different biological problems without any reliable or proven pathology. Could it be that the frenzied pursuit of finding a pathology or etiology without ever objectively defining or understanding the alleged illness is more a means of maintaining a theory than it is an altruistic and scientific endeavor? Psychiatrist and historian Ed Shorter admits,

---

[187] Ibid., 105-6.

[188] Ibid., 89-90.

> Psychiatrists have an obvious self-interest in pathologizing human behavior and have been willing to draw the pathology line ever lower in their efforts to tear as much counseling as possible away from competing psychologists and social workers.[189]

If deception, rather than the outworking behavior, is acknowledged to be the genuine underlying problem, then the continued attempt to medicalize human mindsets and their manifested behavior becomes unnecessary and obstructs the seemingly elusive remedy. These three constructs of mental illness, which psychiatrists view as some of the most serious mental illnesses and which are often referred to as psychosis, share the same core problem: false fixed beliefs and perceptions.

Unipolar Depression

Not only are the constructs of schizophrenia, bipolar, and dissociative disorders not distinct problems, but neither is there a strong difference between unipolar and bipolar depression. As with the other psychiatric disorders, unipolar depression carries with it a false view of self, relationships, and life. Psychologist Richard Bentall comments on how depression is regularly based on false beliefs:

> Invariably, psychotic complaints reflect concerns about the self, or relationships with other people. Psychotically depressed people, for example, often *believe* that they are inadequate, or guilty of imaginary misdeeds. Manic patients, in contrast, often *feel* that they are superior to others, and are capable of achievements that will amaze the world [emphasis added].[190]

"Psychotically depressed" describes those who have false beliefs about themselves which bring them low, whereas those who are "manic" have false beliefs about who they are which reflect a high opinion of themselves. The *DSM-5* describes one common criteria of "major depressive disorder" to be "feelings of worthlessness or excessive or inappropriate guilt (which may be

---

[189] Shorter, *A History of Psychiatry*, 289.

[190] Bentall, *Madness Explained*, 204.

delusional) nearly every day."[191] This description is why the state of depression is historically viewed as the inability or refusal to accept reality. Historian Roy Porter comments on Aretaeus' (one of the most regarded Greek physicians from the first century) view of depression: "For Aretaeus, depression was a grave condition, its delusions, obsessions, and *idees fixes* highly destructive."[192] Interestingly enough, scientific research has revealed that a large percentage of those labeled as having unipolar depression (e.g., major depression) experience mania just as those labeled as having bipolar depression.[193] In an article published in the *Psychiatric Times* in 2017, Chris Aiken remarked that "manic symptoms during unipolar depression are more common than thought."[194] Other studies show that a large percentage of people allegedly "convert from unipolar depression to bipolar depression.[195] But the APA insists in the *DSM-5* that in order to be diagnosed as having major depression the person must meet the criteria that "there has never been a manic episode or a hypomanic episode."[196] The alleged major distinction between unipolar and bipolar depression is not as clear-cut as psychiatrists once believed. Could it be that the true distinction between these constructs rests in how people perceive or believe themselves to be related to reality? Such

---

191 APA, *DSM-5*, 161.

192 Porter, *Madness*, 46.

193 G. H. Vázquez, M. Lolich, C. Cabrera, et al. "Mixed Symptoms in Major Depressive and Bipolar Disorders: A Systematic Review," *Journal of Affective Disorders* 225 (2018): 756-60.

194 Chris Aiken, "The Year in Bipolar: 7 Practice-Changing Papers form 2017," *Psychiatric Times Online* (December 8, 2017): http://www.psychiatrictimes.com/bipolar-disorder/year-bipolar-7-practice-changing-papers-2017/page/0/4.

195 A. Ratheesh, C. Davey, S. Hetrick, et al., "A Systematic Review and Meta-Analysis of Prospective Transition from Major Depression to Bipolar Disorder," *Acta Psychiatry Scandonavian* 135 (2017): 273-84.

196 APA, *DSM-5*, 161.

understanding would explain the different reactions to hopelessness and sorrow observed in people's behavior.

Obsessive-Compulsive Disorder

Obsessive-Compulsive Disorder (OCD) is another specific delusion in which a person falsely believes that non-related behavior can control outcomes of an out-of-control circumstance. The *DSM* describes the construct:

> Recurrent and persistent thoughts, urges, or images that are experienced, at some time during the disturbance, as intrusive and unwanted, and that in most individuals cause marked anxiety or distress. The individual attempts to ignore or suppress such thoughts, urges, or images, to neutralize them with some other thought or action. . . . *These behaviors or mental acts are not connected in a realistic way with what they are designed to neutralize or prevent, or are clearly excessive* [emphasis added].[197]

Rather than invest their energy into working toward solving a problem, people whom psychiatrists label as OCD attempt to control the outcome of their struggle by exerting effort and repetitive behavior into non-related endeavors. Their delusion is thinking that they can control life by their obsessive behavior (what they seemingly can control). While this delusion and its outworking behavior may seem odd when taken to extremes, it is in fact a common human delusion. Many people believe that wearing a lucky shirt or sitting in a specific chair in a certain way during a sports game will allow their favorite team to win. Some sports professionals believe that not shaving will enable them to become champions, while others believe that in order to have a good day, they must drive a certain route, give a high five to a specific employee, or wear certain clothing. Who of us could forget the childhood game of not stepping on a crack in the pavement, lest "we break our mother's back"? Thinking deceptively in these ways can easily become habit, negatively alter the brain, and eventually turn into obsessions.

---

[197] APA, *DSM-5*, 237.

The *DSM* also suggests that the content and severity of false beliefs determine the diagnosis:

> If an individual with obsessive-compulsive disorder is completely convinced that his or her *obsessive-compulsive disorder beliefs are true*, then the diagnosis of obsessive-compulsive disorder, with absent insight/delusional beliefs specifier, should be given rather than a diagnosis of delusional disorder.[198]

OCD is merely a specific false belief that millions of people struggle with.

Anxiety and Somatic Symptom Disorders

The psychiatric concepts found in the various "anxiety disorders" represent further constructs of mental illness that expose false fixed belief as the core of madness. The *DSM-5* states,

> Anxiety disorders include disorders that share features of excessive fear and anxiety and related behavioral disturbances. *Fear is the emotional response to real or perceived imminent threat, whereas anxiety is anticipation of future threat.* . . . While the anxiety disorders tend to be highly comorbid with each other, *they can be differentiated by* close examination of the types of situations that are feared or avoided and the *content of the associated thoughts or beliefs*. [emphases added][199]

Anxiety is the fear of something that is possible. As with the alleged severe disorders, it is the content of beliefs that determines what type of anxiety disorder psychiatrists assign to their counselees.

For example, what the APA once called hypochondria is now called "illness anxiety disorder" under "somatic symptom disorders." The APA explains,

> Most individuals with hypochondriasis are now classified as having somatic symptom disorder; however, in a minority of cases, the diagnosis of *illness anxiety disorder* applies instead [emphasis added]. Illness anxiety disorder entails a preoccupation with having or acquiring a serious, undiagnosed medical illness (Criterion A). Somatic

---

[198] Ibid., 93.

[199] Ibid., 189.

symptoms are not present or, if present, are only mild in intensity (Criterion B). A thorough evaluation fails to identify a serious medical condition that accounts for the individual's concerns.[200]

How ironic, being anxious about one's health without any valid biological marker present is a false belief considered by the APA to be a disease without any biological marker. This same struggle with anxiety about one's health, however, is not unique to anxiety disorders; it is listed in the *DSM-5* under the schizophrenia spectrum as "somatic delusions."[201] The APA later remarks about people diagnosed as having illness anxiety that

> because they believe that they are medically ill, individuals with illness anxiety disorder are encountered far more frequently in medical than in mental health settings.[202]

There is even listed under somatic symptom disorders "Factitious Disorder," which amounts to

> (A) Falsification of physical or psychological signs or symptoms, or induction of injury or disease, associated with identified deception. (B) The individual presents himself or herself to others as ill, impaired, or injured.[203]

Professor of Clinical Psychiatry Sean Spence discusses how evaluating deception in others is central to psychiatric practice and comments on the constructs of malingering and hysteria,

> Consider the distinction between feigned physical symptoms ('malingering') and those ascribed to conversion disorder ('hysteria'). These diagnoses have very different meanings, yet what objective grounds are there for differentiating between them? Notwithstanding the findings of brain imaging experiments, it would seem that, phenomenologically, there is little objective evidence that would favour one above the other, and the diagnosis reached may be influenced by circumstantial factors and the physician's opinion of the patient's personality or background. Also, the subtle 'tricks' used to elicit hysterical motor inconsistency (e.g. the unintentional movement of the 'paralysed' limb) might just as well be used to indicate

---

[200] Ibid., 315.

[201] Ibid., 87.

[202] Ibid., 316.

[203] Ibid., 324.

> deception. The point is not that these disorders are equivalent, rather that they lack objective differentiation.[204]

All of the alleged eating disorders, personality disorders, paraphilic disorders, dissociative disorders, substance abuse disorders, somatic disorders, and anxiety disorders share false fixed beliefs, and these false fixed beliefs are the true substance of numerous alleged mental illnesses.

Gender Dysphoria

The psychiatric disorder of *gender dysphoria* describes someone who has

> a marked incongruence between the gender they have been assigned to (usually at birth, referred to as natal gender) and their experienced/expressed gender [their belief about themselves]. This discrepancy is the core component of the diagnosis.[205]

The American College of Pediatrics declared in 2017 that this alleged disorder is simply a specific delusion:

> The American College of Pediatricians urges healthcare professionals, educators and legislators to reject all policies that condition children to accept as normal a life of chemical and surgical impersonation of the opposite sex. Facts - not ideology - determine reality.[206]

The American College of Pediatrics also suggests,

> When an otherwise healthy biological boy believes he is a girl, or an otherwise healthy biological girl believes she is a boy, an objective psychological problem exists that lies in the mind not the body, and it should be treated as such. These children suffer from gender dysphoria. Gender dysphoria (GD), formerly listed as Gender Identity Disorder (GID), is a recognized mental disorder in the most recent

---

[204] Sean A. Spence, "The Deceptive Brain," *Journal of the Royal Society of Medicine* 97, no. 1 (2004): 6.

[205] APA, *DSM-5*, 453.

[206] "Gender Ideology Harms Children," *American College of Pediatrics Online* (January 2017): https://www.acpeds.org/the-college-speaks/position-statements/gender-ideology-harms-children.

> edition of the Diagnostic and Statistical Manual of the American Psychiatric Association (*DSM-5*).[207]

A false belief that contradicts clear empirical evidence is the underlying problem in those said to have gender dysphoria; there is a discrepancy between their feeling and reality. This false belief causes them "dysphoria" or distress.

The APA has chosen to make dysphoria—"to be dissatisfied"—their greatest concern and not the fact that a person is delusional about their physical nature:

> *Gender dysphoria* refers to the distress that may accompany the incongruence between one's experienced or expressed gender and one's assigned gender. . . . The current term [*gender dysphoria*] is more descriptive than the previous *DSM-IV* term *gender identity disorder* and focuses on dysphoria as the clinical problem, not identity per se.[208]

Other physicians also remark in an article published in the *New England Journal of Medicine*,

> *The Diagnostic and Statistical Manual of Mental Disorders* uses the term *gender dysphoria* to describe the clinically significant distress that, for many transgender people, accompanies a profound misalignment between gender identity and assigned sex at birth. The current standard of care for treating gender dysphoria is gender transition, which may include mental health counseling, hormone therapy, and reconstructive surgeries affecting primary and secondary sex characteristics. . . . Transgender people's need for care that affirms their true selves and promotes their health and well-being parallels all Americans' desire for high-quality, affordable health insurance coverage and health care.[209]

In the case of gender dysphoria, the APA has chosen to view the distress that having false fixed beliefs produces as the mental illness rather than identifying the actual delusions as problematic. In turn, they suggest leading the client into further deception (mentally and physically) in order to allegedly treat

---

[207] Ibid.

[208] APA, *DSM-5*, 451.

[209] Kellan E. Baker, "The Future of Transgender Coverage," *New England Journal of Medicine* (May 11, 2017): http://www.nejm.org/doi/full/10.1056/NEJMp1702427?query=TOC&.

the false fixed beliefs, and they advocate that society should also accept a known delusion as if it were truth.

But one could just as easily consider the delusional thinking found in the construct of gender dysphoria as evidence of schizophrenia. The APA recognizes this fact and acknowledges that "schizophrenia (or other psychotic disorders) and gender dysphoria may co-occur."[210] The APA insists that these disorders are different, yet they both expose delusions/false fixed beliefs to be the genuine problem. Gender dysphoria is said to typically lacks hallucinations as a criterion, though the deception is regularly sensory as well. Still, false beliefs are foundational to both psychiatric constructs.

Comorbidity

The example of gender dysphoria highlights a key component in the APA's classification system of madness presented in the *DSM-5*. When a person's delusions fit multiple diagnoses, the construct of mental illness that best describes the content of the false beliefs will typically be assigned. If a delusion's content fits numerous constructs of mental illness (and they mostly do), then clinicians may choose to diagnose multiple disorders (comorbidity). Comorbidity is not a disorder itself; rather it is a medical term applied by physicians when more than one disease is discovered in patients (e.g., a patient has both cancer and Alzheimer's disease).

In constructs of mental illness, comorbidity is the norm, and almost every disorder in the *DSM-5* lists scores of comorbid disorders. For example, the construct of "major depressive disorder" "co-occurs" with numerous other constructs:

> Other disorders with which major depressive disorder frequently co-occurs are substance-related disorders, panic disorder, obsessive-

---

[210] APA, *DSM-5*, 458.

compulsive disorder, anorexia nervosa, bulimia nervosa, and borderline personality disorder.[211]

In constructs of mental illness, comorbidity does not identify the existence of numerous diseases as it does in valid medical conditions. Instead, comorbidity or co-occurrence identifies numerous false beliefs and their corresponding behaviors. If people are deceived, they will most likely be deceived in numerous ways and have numerous false beliefs.

The APA's tendency to classify delusions as separate disease entities based on their content and subsequent behavior does not determine that gender dysphoria, bipolar disorder, delusional disorder, schizotypal personality disorder, or any other psychiatric constructs are unique forms of madness or any different than psychosis. It simply means that specific ways in which people are commonly deceived and subsequently behave have been identified, framed, and categorized as different forms of madness. It is the content and pattern of delusions which determines the differential diagnosis.

Madness, even in the psychiatric paradigm, remains a problem with false fixed beliefs. This understanding is consistent with ancient biblical descriptions of madness, and such similarity of definition indicates that faith may in fact be more relevant to modern psychiatric discussions than commonly thought.

From the clear definition of the modern concept of madness naturally arise several important related questions that need to be answered: (1) If the vast majority of alleged types of mental illnesses amount to false fixed beliefs, then is there simply one form of madness with different manifestations or are their many kinds? (2) Is deception/false fixed beliefs part of our human nature or an abnormality? (3) If false fixed beliefs are normative, then at what point do they become delusions/madness or are all false fixed beliefs forms of madness? (4) Who has the authority to decide what beliefs are true and what are false? (5) Are all

---

[211] Ibid., 168.

constructs of mental illness delusions or has the APA redefined madness to accommodate its ever-changing beliefs about human nature? The remainder of the book will focus on answering these important questions.

CONCLUSION

From the first recorded episode to today's psychiatric constructs, it is clear that humanity has defined madness or lunacy as a departure from truth/reality. Most people accept deception or false fixed beliefs as normal, yet when we individually or collectively believe false fixed beliefs to be extravagant, disturbing, threatening, uncomfortable, or—in our estimation—too grand to be explained or reasoned by our own faith and knowledge, we tend to call them *madness*.

The Christian Bible and the psychiatric bible (*DSM-5*) are, to many people, the most important sources in considering how to define madness or mental illness. Incredibly, these two bookends in the history of madness—though their worldviews are antithetical—provide a unified core feature of madness from which to form an objective definition.

Despite the claim of scientific advancement, the *DSM-5* has not replaced the biblical definition of madness; it simply suggests a new way of interpreting and treating the soul's deceived condition. This belief maintains that the "brain [is] the seat of mental illness, and that a medical approach to the brain could replace purely spiritual theories."[212] While the psychiatric definition shares the core elements of madness presented in Scripture, the APA has rejected the Bible's description of human nature and specifically the soul/psyche. Instead of viewing the soul as spiritual and unapproachable through the scientific method, psychiatric theorists insist that the brain is the seat of

---

212 Group for the Advancement of Psychiatry, "The History of Psychiatry 19th Century," 3:35-44.

the mind and that the soul's condition (psychosis) is a medical problem.[213]

A definition of madness or mental illness, then, not only reflects a person whose mindsets, words, and behaviors are discerned to be false, but it also exposes the beliefs about anthropology, normalcy, and truth in the one who insists that others are mad. Both the faith of the one being labeled as mad and the perspective of the person(s) judging others to be mad are most certainly equal considerations. In this way, madness is a construct that attempts to explain how people relate to truth/reality or life according to their worldview.

---

213 Ibid.

CHAPTER 4

RECOGNIZING MADNESS

"Madness is as madness looks."[214]
Roy Porter, historian

"Madness is something that frightens and fascinates us all. It is a word with which we are universally familiar, and a condition that haunts the human imagination . . . . A whole industry has grown up, devoted to its management and suppression."[215]
Andrew Scull, historian

Not only has the core of insanity remained the same throughout history, but so also have the criteria used by all approaches to identify or diagnose madness. Whether it is a pastor, a therapist, a shaman, a physician, or a family member diagnosing another as being deeply deceived, they must each discern the content of a person's mind by evaluating that person's speech and behavior.

A PROBLEM IN THINKING

More than any other identifiable element, a problem in one's thinking has been recognized throughout history as characterizing madness. In fact, the idea of madness, lunacy,

---

214 Porter, *Madness*, 63.

215 Scull, *Madness*, 1.

insanity, or mental illness has historically conveyed the idea of an unhealthy mind or irrational/unreasonable thought. The term *sanity* comes from the Latin word *sanus*—meaning health. In Scripture, the metaphor of sickness is also utilized to illustrate just how impaired and terminal all people are in their deception (e.g., Jeremiah 17:9). Historically, to be insane meant that the person was thinking in a way that impaired or destroyed the health of the soul, the body, or the society.

The ancient Romans had several phrases to describe insanity. "*Non compos* [or *compotes*] *mentis*,"[216] for example, was a phrase that described someone who was "not entirely there" mentally, "not in a right mind,"[217] or someone with an "unsound mind."[218] To be insane was fundamentally a mental problem.[219] The phrase *mens sana in corpora sano* is also significant, since it translates as "a healthy mind in a healthy body." Until the acceptance of biological psychiatrists' theory of materialism (which in the early 1800s proposed that the mind was merely a byproduct of a person's brain/biology),[220] the mind was understood by most to be a non-physical part of humanity which had the power to control and alter a person's physical nature. Likewise, the mind's condition—when irrational and delusional—was not typically viewed as a medical issue. Historian Andrew Scull explains,

> Madness is not a medical term (though it was once widely used by medical men). It is a commonsense category, reflecting our culture's

---

216 Ray, *Medical Jurisprudence of Insanity*, 4-6.

217 Daniel N. Robinson, *An Intellectual History of Psychology* (Madison, WI: University of Wisconsin Press, 1995), 305.

218 Ray, *Medical Jurisprudence of Insanity*, 4.

219 The term *comprehension*—understanding the whole—is derived from the word *compos*.

220 *Materialism* and *positivism* are virtually the same philosophy: "Providing psychiatry with a sound scientific basis was particularly important at that time, on account of its strong positivistic and Darwinian leanings" (Porter, *Madness*, 183).

> (every culture's?) recognition that unreason exists, that some of our number seem not to share our mental universe: they are 'irrational'; they are emotionally withdrawn, downcast, or raging; their disorderly minds exhibit extremes of incomprehensible and uncontrollable extravagance and incoherence, or the grotesquely denuded mental life of the demented.[221]

At its core, madness was and still remains a problem of the mind.

Thoughts Can Be Unhealthy

Negative impairing thoughts from the immaterial mind first and foremost characterize mental illness. More specifically, madness can only be recognized by discerning whether thoughts are healthy ("a sound mind") or unhealthy ("an unsound mind"[222]). This medicinal metaphor distinguishes what is true from what is false, which may be why Ralph Waldo Emerson once stated that "every violation of truth is not only a sort of suicide in the liar but is a stab at the health of human society."[223] Thoughts or beliefs which are false are, from every perspective, considered to be harmful and destructive to individuals and society.

The Mind's Non-Material Nature

The need to evaluate the mind (specifically a person's beliefs) in order to determine its health, coupled with very real human limitation in doing so, is largely responsible for the many confusing theories and controversies produced in the last 200 years. The immaterial nature of the mind has historically posed tremendous problems for people to approach and remedy madness and more recently to define it. The mind/psyche/soul—what many humanistic professionals today refer to as

---

221 Scull, *Madness*, 2.

222 Ray, *Medical Jurisprudence of Insanity*, 6.

223 Ralph Waldo Emerson: http://quodid.com/quotes/1077/ralph-waldo-emerson/every-violation-of-truth-is-not-only-a.

"consciousness"[224]—cannot be observed, and the incorporeal nature of the mind is one of the key characteristics of mental illness.[225] Former president of the APA Jeffrey Lieberman comments that madness was and still is a concept that is distinguished from valid neurological problems which have measurable biological markers:

> The discovery that some mental disorders had a recognizable biological basis—while other did not—led to the establishment of two distinct disciplines. Physicians who specialized exclusively in disorders with an observable neural stamp became known as neurologists. Those who dealt with the invisible disorders of the mind became known as psychiatrists.[226]

He continues,

> Psychiatry originated as a medical specialty that took as its province a set of maladies that, *by their very definition, had no identifiable physical cause* [emphasis added]. Appropriately, the term "psychiatry"—coined by the German physician Johann Christian Reil in 1808—literally means "medical treatment of the soul." Like the Bering Strait, the schism between the neurological brain and the psychiatric soul separated two continents of medical practice. Again and again over the next two centuries, psychiatrists would declare fraternity and equality with their neurological counterparts across the border, then just as abruptly proclaim liberty from them, insisting that the ineffable mind was the field of greater truth.[227]

By definition, mental illness is "invisible" and has "no identifiable physical cause." Mental illness not only has no physical cause, but it is also not a real disease. The once-prominent Allen Frances remarks on how mental illnesses are constructs that attempt to explain human nature: "We saw *DSM-IV* as a guidebook, not a bible—*a collection of temporarily useful*

---

224 Francis Crick, *The Astonishing Hypothesis: The Scientific Search for the Soul* (New York: Simon and Schuster, 1995), preface I.

225 The *DSM-5* contains several valid neurodegenerative diseases (e.g., Alzheimer's, dementia, and autism) which are included as mental disorders. These are valid physical diseases/impairments with biological markers and should not be considered as mental illnesses.

226 Lieberman, *Shrinks*, 26

227 Ibid., 26-27.

diagnostic constructs, not a catalog of 'real' diseases [emphasis added]."[228] The mind itself is an incorporeal reality; therefore, the scientific method is useless in studying the mind/soul/psyche and causes of mental illness.

So, within psychiatric thinking, the mind must either be diminished in its significance, theoretically reduced to a function of the brain, or explained as somehow equaling observable behavior. Dr. Candace Pert notes,

> Measurement! It is the very foundation of the modern scientific method, the means by which the material world is admitted into existence. Unless we can measure something, science won't concede it exists, which is why science refuses to deal with such "nonthings" as the emotions, the mind, the soul, or the spirit.[229]

Unhealthy thoughts simply cannot be observed or measured with scientific methods. More specifically as it relates to defining madness, a person's beliefs, faith, and perceptions cannot be physically observed. The psychiatric construct of madness known today as schizophrenia illustrates this point:

> It is readily agreed that 'schizophrenia' is unobservable, an abstract concept inferred from overt behavior or from verbal reports of behaviour and experience (Kendell, 1991; APA, 1994).[230]

The mind's product (behavior) and physical effects can, however, both be observed and interpreted. But the mind itself cannot be seen and neurological and genetic studies have yielded no validating or reliable markers to explain a person's faith. Drs. Parnask, Sass, and Zahavi comment,

> Consciousness and experience are typically treated as if they were somehow on a par with other spatial-temporal, substantive objects of the natural world (i.e., things)—ie [sic], as if conscious events (such as delusions or auditory hallucinations) were well-delimited, atomic

---

[228] Frances, *Saving Normal*, 73.

[229] Candace Pert, *Molecules of Emotion*, 21.

[230] Boyle, *Schizophrenia*, 2.

> entities that could be easily captured and quantified without much concern for more contextually based or Gestalt-like features.[231]

The historian Andrew Scull also notes:

> For despite the fact that contemporary psychiatry seeks to promulgate a notion of madness as the external manifestation of a badly wired brain, the consequence of faulty biochemistry or an excess or deficiency of certain neurotransmitters, the process of drawing boundaries around the mad remains an uncertain and contested activity, the site of recurrent controversy that only occasionally has analogues in other branches of medicine. No X-rays, no PET scans, no laboratory tests exist that unambiguously pronounce that one is sane, this one mad.[232]

The APA also recognizes that no biological markers exist to validate any speculated disorder of mental illness contained in the *DSM-5*, and they cannot wait until "incontrovertible etiological or pathophysiological mechanisms are identified to fully validate specific disorders or disorder spectra."[233] What, then, do biological psychiatrists and psychologists do when no biological markers exist to determine madness? Ashley Pettus asserts in *Harvard Magazine*:

> Without clear biological markers, researchers and clinicians must rely on interviews to assess the occurrence and severity of mental disorders. Interview questions follow criteria from the *Diagnostic and Statistical Manual of Mental Disorders* (*DSM*)—a 1,000-page volume *covering the gamut of human affect and behavior*, from mood and personality to sexuality and addiction. Researchers have arrived at the syndromes listed in the *DSM* by tracking symptoms and symptom clusters, with particular attention to duration, age of onset, family prevalence, gender distribution, and response to treatment. Now in its revised fourth edition, the *DSM* has provided the field with a common language for identifying and discussing the enormous range of mental-health problems, *yet it remains more a proximate description than a verifiable picture of reality* [emphasis added].[234]

---

[231] Josef Parnask, Louis A. Sass, and Dan Zahavi, "Rediscovering Psychopathology: The Epistemology and Phenomenology of the Psychiatric Object," *Schizophrenia Bulletin* 39, no. 2 (2013): 270-77.

[232] Scull, *Madness*, 4.

[233] APA, *DSM-5*, 20.

[234] Pettus, "Psychiatry by Prescription."

Without biological markers and pathologies, attempting to provide a biological or scientific approach and a definition of mental illness amounts to subjective faith and conjecture. As a result, materialists insist that mental illness cannot be objectively defined, and behaviors are classified in the *DSM* as imprecisely defining alleged mental illnesses. Dogmatically defining mental illness as being biologically caused without biological markers, pathology, or scientific means to study faith and deception amounts to speculative beliefs. Still, the spurious claim that madness is biologically caused continues to be made as if it has been proved or will be soon with empirical evidence. Without the ability to empirically observe the immaterial mind or its faith, scientific and medical tools will always fail to explain the origins, true nature, and remedy for false beliefs.

Though the doctrines of Christianity and materialism both agree that unhealthy thinking (false fixed beliefs) is at the core of madness, materialism is an attempt to dismiss biblical explanations of humanity and specifically the immaterial soul and human morality. Evolutionary biologist and geneticist at Harvard University, Richard Lewontin explains,

> Our willingness to accept scientific claims that are against common sense is the key to an understanding of the real struggle between science and the supernatural. We take the side of science in spite of the patent absurdity of some of its constructs, in spite of its failure to fulfill many of its extravagant promises of health and life, in spite of the tolerance of the scientific community of unsubstantiated just so stories, because we have a prior commitment, a commitment to materialism. It is not that the methods of and institutions of science somehow compel us to accept a material explanation of the phenomenal world, but on the contrary, that we are forced by our a priori adherence to material causes to create an apparatus of investigation and a set of concepts that produce material explanations, no matter how counterintuitive, no matter how mystifying to the uninitiated. *Moreover, that materialism is absolute, for we cannot allow a Divine Foot in the door* [emphasis added]."[235]

---

[235] Richard C. Lewontin, "Billions and Billions of Demons," review of *The Demon-Haunted World: Science as a Candle in the Dark*, by Carl Sagan, *New York Review of Books*, January 7, 1997, 31.

Materialism is simply one belief system used to explain human nature and interpret thoughts and behavior, and it is the primary belief system that must be utilized to insist that the mind is a physical reality or the product of the brain. The historian of madness Roy Porter notes how Thomas Hobbes's (1588-1679) idea of materialism was posited as an attempt to dismiss religious beliefs:

> Hobbes deemed the universe a material continuum, utterly devoid of spirit, under a God who was characterized primarily by power. . . . This *materialist reading of human action* as moved entirely by external sense-inputs permitted Hobbes to dismiss religious beliefs about spirits and witches as hallucinations spawned by the fevered operations of the brain. By extension, religion itself was a form of delusion. Insanity was thus erroneous thought caused by some defect in the body's machinery.[236]

Porter's remarks reveal that materialism represents a "reading" or interpretation of "human action" or behavior.[237] If one understands that an underlying problem of behavior is in the mind, yet that person is unwilling to accept the reality that the mind is immaterial/spiritual and exists on its own, then looking for environmental or biological markers and etiologies (measurable and observable components) becomes vital to sustain beliefs. Editor in Chief of the *Psychiatric Times* Ronald Pies details this widely accepted modern materialistic belief in an article titled, "Hearing Voices and Psychiatry's (Real) Medical Model":

> In so far as human emotion, cognition, and behavior are mediated by brain function, there is always an inherent biological foundation to dysfunctional states, such as clinical depression, psychosis etc. Valid psychosocial and cultural explanations of human experiences do not nullify (or contradict) the biological foundations of these experiences. . . . That certain human experiences or perceptions (e.g., "voices") have a

---

236 Porter, *Madness*, 59.

237 Since Hobbes rejected the supernatural, he insisted that religion itself was a delusion, a form of madness, a false fixed belief. If the beliefs of an authority or perceived authority do not agree with another's faith (even false faith), then such power enables madness to be a social control mechanism.

> discernible "meaning," symbolism, or psychological significance to the patient does not mean they have no neuropathological etiology.[238]

If a person's perspective is narrowly fixed on scientific study (only that which can be seen), then addressing the immaterial mind and its thoughts and beliefs and attempts to accurately define madness will inevitably fail. It is no wonder that many biological psychiatrists who refuse to accept the mind as immaterial, separate from the brain, and able to control moral executive functions of the body insist that mental illness cannot be defined and try to connect every aspect of human nature to a physical etiology.

The Mind's Non-Material Problem

Both the ancient Jewish and Roman understanding that a person's thoughts directly affect the health of the body is increasingly accepted among many of today's prominent physicians. Former chief of brain biochemistry at the National Institutes of Health[239] (one of the highest neuroscientific achievements possible) and current Professor of Physiology and Biophysics at Georgetown University Medical Center, Dr. Candace Pert exemplifies this position:

> A growing number of scientists recognize that we are in the midst of a scientific revolution, a major paradigm shift with tremendous implications for how we deal with health and disease. The Cartesian era, as Western philosophical thought since Descartes has been known, has been dominated by reductionist methodology, which attempts to understand life by examining the tiniest pieces of it, and then extrapolating from those pieces to overarching surmises about the whole. Reductionist Cartesian thought is now in the process of adding something very new and exciting—and holistic. As I've watched as well as participated in this process, I've come to believe that virtually

---

[238] Ronald W. Pies, "Hearing Voices and Psychiatry's (Real) Medical Model," *Psychiatric Times Online* (September 4, 2017): http://www.psychiatrictimes.com/schizophrenia/hearing-voices-and-psychiatrys-real-medical-model.

[239] Candace B. Pert, *Molecules of Emotion: The Science Behind Mind-Body Medicine* (New York: Scribner, 1997), 14.

> all illness, if not psychosomatic in foundation, has a definite psychosomatic component.[240]

Those physicians embracing and participating in this scientific revolution are not creating a new paradigm, though; they are rather returning to a previously understood medical position that non-physical mental states directly alter the physical body and its function. Dr. Pert rightly acknowledges this return to ancient anthropology as a "paradigm shift." She explains further,

> We are all in denial about the importance of psychosomatic causes of illness. Break the word *psychosomatic* down into its parts, and it becomes *psyche*, meaning mind or soul, and *soma*, meaning body. Though the fact that they are fused into one word suggests some kind of connection between the two, that connection is anathema in much of our culture. For many of us, and certainly for most of the medical establishment, bringing the mind too close to the body threatens the legitimacy of any particular illness, suggesting it may be imaginary, unreal, *unscientific*. If psychological contributions to physical health and disease are viewed with suspicion, the suggestion that the soul—literal translation of psyche—might matter is considered downright absurd. For now we are getting into the mystical realm, where scientists have been officially forbidden to tread ever since the seventeenth century.[241]

But Pert does not stop there; she elaborates on her scientific theory of how the mind directly affects the body:

> We can bring about the release of endorphins through our state of mind. . . . I like to think of mental phenomena as messengers bringing information and intelligence from the nonphysical world to the body, where they manifest via their physical substrate, the neuropeptides and their receptors.[242]

Another neuroscientist also comments on how the mind is not a physical or mechanical reality even if thoughts translate into neurological activity and behavior:

> The main point I want to make is that over the recent years, psychiatry has focused more on a mechanistic approach to psychopathology and

---

240 Ibid., 18.

241 Ibid., 18.

242 Ibid., 311.

> lost any connection to ideas related to a philosophy of mind. A psyche cannot be defined in operational terms, whether or not certain kinds of output of the psyche are being generated by the brain.[243]

Her point is important: even if the brain produces the mind, it is still not operational within the scientific method. The mind is a matter of philosophy or belief and not of scientific study. Therefore, philosophy is required whether the mind is a separate entity from the brain or a phenomenon which the brain produces.

Ancient Rome's understanding that the mind can control and alter the body was not unique to Roman culture. The Bible—where the concept of madness originates—also shares this perspective. For example, Proverbs 3:7-8 states, "Be not wise in your own eyes; fear the Lord, and turn away from evil. It will be healing to your flesh and refreshment to your bones." Proverbs 17:22 provides another illustration: "A joyful heart is good medicine, but a crushed spirit [depression; hopelessness] dries up the bones." A person's beliefs and thoughts directly affect the physical body, and when someone's thoughts are continually false, then there will also exist negative biological symptoms. For example, the *DSM-5* states how neuroscientific studies show differentials exist in the brains of those diagnosed as having schizophrenia:

> Differences are evident in multiple brain regions between groups of healthy individuals and persons with schizophrenia, including evidence from neuroimaging, neuropathological, and neurophysiological studies. Differences are also evident in cellular architecture, white matter connectivity, and gray matter volume in a variety of regions such as the prefrontal and temporal cortices. Reduced overall brain volume has been observed, as well as increased brain volume reduction with age.[244]

---

243 "Mary Anne" comments on an article written by Ronald W. Pies, "Hearing Voices and Psychiatry's (Real) Medical Model," *Psychiatric Times Online* (September 4, 2017): http://www.psychiatrictimes.com/articles/hearing-voices-and-psychiatrys-real-medical-model/page/0/2.

244 APA, *DSM-5*, 101-102.

Materialists frame these differences as causative and validating proof of the construct of schizophrenia, but these conclusions are based on their presuppositional belief.

There is a great amount of empirical evidence, however, to conclude that brain differentials are effects of deceitful thinking and not causative. For instance, in an article published in 2016, numerous universities (including Duke University and University College London) together conducted controlled scientific studies which utilized neuroimaging to measure deception's impact on the brain. What they found in their research was that the more a person repeated deceptive thoughts or was dishonest, the more deceived they became and the more their brains atrophied in response:

> Dishonesty is an integral part of our social world, influencing domains ranging from finance and politics to personal relationships. Anecdotally, digressions from a moral code are often described as a series of small breaches that grow over time. Here we provide empirical evidence for a gradual escalation of self-serving dishonesty and reveal a neural mechanism supporting it. *Behaviorally, we show that the extent to which participants engage in self-serving dishonesty increases with repetition. Using functional MRI, we show that signal reduction in the amygdala is sensitive to the history of dishonest behavior, consistent with adaptation* [emphasis added]. Critically, the extent of reduced amygdala sensitivity to dishonesty on a present decision relative to the previous one predicts the magnitude of escalation of self-serving dishonesty on the next decision. The findings uncover a biological mechanism that supports a 'slippery slope': what begins as small acts of dishonesty can escalate into larger transgressions.[245]

While materialistic scientists attempt to interpret the results according to their beliefs, they in truth, expose that deceptive thinking alters the brain in impairing and observable ways. In other words, the brain is not causing false beliefs; it is affected by the mind's deceit.

These findings help to explain how people can become psychotic; they simply repeat false beliefs—attempting to dissociate from their situations—until they are spiritually and

---

245 Neil Garrett, Stephanie C. Lazzaro, Dan Ariely, and Tali Sharot, "The Brain Adapts to Dishonesty," *Nature Neuroscience*, October 24, 2016 doi:10.1038/nn.4426.

physically overwhelmed by deceit. Neuroscientists understand that the people diagnosed with schizophrenia have altered brains, but they are unsure of what causes these alterations:

> It appears that neuroimaging data has confirmed the expectation that hallucinations involve altered activity in the neural circuitry known to be involved in normal audition and language and their control. However, the major question of how this altered activity arises is still unanswered.[246]

The findings of repetitive deceptive thinking's impact on the brain may very well expose that hallucinations are simply by-products of false belief's ongoing effects on the brain.

Often times, hallucinations are triggered by something external (like a song or a sound) which causes a person to engage in familiar deceptive thinking. Yet, as psychologist Adrian Furnham acknowledges, hallucinations are fundamentally a false belief:

> Hallucinatory episodes may follow a pattern: first, something like a particular memory or sound sparks off the hallucination. The person then tests if it's real and begins to believe it is. The fantasy, distortion, and unreality continues and grows and gets confused with actual perception.[247]

The more people embrace falsehood, the more their brains are negatively affected, and, as a result, specific memories, how they perceive environments, and the quality of their relationships can easily become distorted. As we observed in chapter three, hallucinations are not disconnected phenomena from a person's history or character.

To further illustrate how the spiritual nature—through relationships—can alter the physical nature, one need only to study how talk therapy (psychotherapy) can also alter the nervous system. Though deceit can negatively alter the brain (a

---

[246] Patricia Boksa, "On the Neurobiology of Hallucinations," *Journal of Psychiatry & Neuroscience* 34, no. 4 (2009): 260–62.

[247] Adrian Furnham, "Why We Hallucinate: The 5 Most Common Causes, and 3 Primary Theories," *Psychology Today Onlin,* June 2, 2015, https://www.psychologytoday.com/blog/sideways-view/201506/why-we-hallucinate.

process that I refer to as neurodestructivity), receiving truth repeatedly through a meaningful relationship can positively change the brain (neuroplasticity). As thoughts become more realistic and honest, the brain also changes to reflect these beliefs. Former president of the APA Renee Binder writes,

> Ongoing research has validated the use of psychotherapy as a skill to treat serious mental disorders, and this is unlikely to change, even as we develop more targeted neuroscientifically informed interventions. For example, the recent RAISE research (Recovery After an Initial Schizophrenia Episode) has shown that psychosocial interventions can improve outcomes. In addition, psychotherapy interventions have been shown to alter the circuitry of the brain.[248]

When false beliefs and perspectives change toward truth, so too do neural connections and health. Psychiatrists Samantha Brooks and Dan Stein explain,

> There is abundant and growing experimental evidence that some types of psychotherapy are correlated with changes in the brain which, in turn, are correlated with improvement in the patient's condition. A complete review of this literature is beyond the scope of this response, but several reviews are available. For example, Brooks and Stein performed a systematic review of 19 functional magnetic resonance imaging studies examining the neural bases of cognitive-behavioral therapy (CBT) in 509 patients with anxiety and related disorders. They concluded that "... although each of these related disorders is mediated by somewhat different neural circuitry, CBT may act in a similar way to increase prefrontal control of subcortical structures."[249]

The only way to change false beliefs and heal the brain from deceit's damage is to present truth to the one deceived.

While cognitive behavioral therapy may help people to think truthfully about their lives and positively alter their brains to some extent, it cannot heal humanity's deceptive nature or resolve the greatest destructive consequences of deceit: death.

---

[248] Renee Binder, "Should Psychotherapy Remain Part of Psychiatry?" *Psychiatric News Online*, January 29, 2016, https://psychnews.psychiatryonline .org/doi/full/10.1176/appi.pn.2016.2a11.

[249] Samantha J. Brooks and Dan J. Stein, "A Systematic Review of the Neural Bases of Psychotherapy for Anxiety and Related Disorders," *Dialogues in Clinical Neuroscience* 3 (September 17, 2015): 261-79.

This remedy requires a change of foundational faith/worldview in relation to one's own existence and the existence of God.

It is also important to note that prior to neuroscientific discovery that falsehood negatively alters the physical nature, Scripture first established this fact: In Psalm 32:2, King David states,

> Blessed is the man against whom the LORD counts no iniquity, and *in whose spirit there is no deceit* [emphasis added]. For when I kept silent, my bones wasted away through my groaning all day long.[250]

Both Scripture and scientific evidence attest that false fixed beliefs will inevitability destroy a person's physical and spiritual natures—a point upon which all positions can agree.

In addition to the theory of brain-dysfunction as an attempt to prove an etiology of madness, the theory of genetic disorder has been a popular notion asserted by Emil Kraepelin in the late 1800s. While millions of dollars have been spent in attempt to prove the genetic theory of schizophrenia, it has failed to yield any empirical evidence to validate such a belief. Professor of Neuroanatomy Jonathan Leo remarks,

> The idea that mental illness is the result of a genetic predisposition is the foundation for modern-day psychiatry, and has been the driving force for how we research money is allocated, how patients are treated, and how society views people diagnosed with conditions identified in the *DSM-V*. Schizophrenia holds a unique spot in the annals of mental health research because of its perceived anatomical underpinnings, and is often cited as evidence in favor of a genetic predisposition to other conditions. The logic at work is that if schizophrenia is genetic, then depression, obsessive compulsive disorder, attention deficit hyperactivity disorder (ADHD), and a host of other *DSM-V* conditions must also have their roots in dysfunctional genes.[251]

He later states,

> Yet, in spite of the fact that molecular geneticists have spent countless hours and millions of dollars, a specific gene has never been found . . . .

---

[250] Sin or iniquity is a perversion of truth; it is a clear sign of deceit.

[251] Jonathan Leo, "The Search for Schizophrenia Genes," *Issues in Science and Technology Online*, February 4, 2016, http://issues.org/32-2/the-search-for-schizophrenia-genes/.

> Compared to physical conditions, the debate about genetic risk factors for psychological conditions such as schizophrenia, depression, and ADHD, which all lack distinct biological markers, is even more heated . . . . We now know that biomarkers or specific genes for psychological conditions do not exist, that this research will not lead to magic pharmacological bullets, and that many of our assumptions about mental illness were wrong.[252]

There have been countless studies conducted over the last two centuries attempting to prove a link between mental illness and genetics, but each of them has failed to provide any reliable empirical evidence that shows how false beliefs are empirically connected to genes.[253] In fact, such a connection can never be proved using the scientific method, since beliefs are non-physical aspects of human nature; it is a fallacy to claim that the incorporeal nature of beliefs can be scientifically linked to the physical nature of genes. Such a belief—though it is irrational—is necessary if a person has dogmatically accepted materialism to explain all of human nature.

It is not surprising that clinicians who hold to the Kraepelinian theory of mental illness (the current medical model) have adopted a scientific sounding term to describe the missing link between genes and false beliefs: *endophenotypes*. Professor of Psychiatry at Minnesota Medical School L.L. Gottesman explains,

> Endophenotypes, *measurable components unseen by the unaided eye along the pathway between disease and distal genotype*, have emerged as an important concept in the study of complex neuropsychiatric diseases [emphasis added]. An endophenotype may be neurophysiological, biochemical, endocrinological, neuroanatomical, cognitive, or neuropsychological (including configured self-report data) in nature. Endophenotypes represent simpler clues to genetic underpinnings than the disease syndrome itself, promoting the view that psychiatric

---

252 Ibid.

253 For further study on the genetic theory of schizophrenia, see Berger, *Influence of Nurture*, 54-63.

> diagnoses can be decomposed or deconstructed, which can result in more straightforward-and successful-genetic analysis.[254]

As observed in Gottesman's comments, endophenotypes are not actual things; they are conjecture and "inferred."[255] Sadie Dingfelder remarks in the *Monitor* about the "hunt for endophenotypes":

> Mental illnesses such as bipolar disorder and schizophrenia are very heritable, but the search for culprit genes can seem hopelessly complex. Perhaps dozens contribute to mental illness, and they interact with brain chemistry, brain structures and the environment in a dizzying array of ways. Even more confounding, nearly identical symptoms can result from very different behind-the-scenes malfunctions, researchers say. "[Mental illnesses] as we currently define them are far too complex and far too multifactorial to understand," says Todd Gould, MD, a research fellow at the National Institute of Mental Health's Laboratory of Molecular Pathophysiology. "We need to break down and decompose these disorders into parts that can be more tractable." . . . *Shining a light on these hidden mechanisms*—known as endophenotypes—is a natural fit for psychologists says Gottesman, who introduced the term in the 1970s, along with his colleague James Shields [emphasis added]."[256]

If constructs of mental illnesses are "broken down" or "deconstructed" into their objective realties (i.e., they are defined precisely rather through the lens of speculative beliefs), then it becomes evident that false beliefs can never be scientifically linked to physical genes. The hunt for endophenotypes ("the hidden mechanisms") will go on indefinitely while researchers and theorists simultaneously maintain the false materialistic hope that mental illness is a physical disease with a physical pathology. Endophenotypes are not scientific connections but vital beliefs to sustain "biomythology." Renowned psychiatrist Peter Breggin comments,

---

254 L. L. Gottesman, "The Endophenotype Concept in Psychiatry: Etymology and Strategic Intentions," *American Journal of Psychiatry* 160, no. 4 (April 2003): 636.

255 Ibid.

256 Sadie F. Dingfelder, "The Hunt for Endophenotypes," *Monitor Staff* 37, no. 10 (November 2006), 20.

> In the world of modern psychiatry, claims can become truth, hopes can become achievements, and propaganda is taken as science. Nowhere is this more obvious than in psychiatric pretensions concerning the genetics, biology, and physical treatment of depression and mania. As also found in regard to neuroleptics and so-called schizophrenia, biopsychiatric research is based too often on distortions, incomplete information, and sometimes outright fraud—at the expense of reason and science.[257]

Starting from a wrong presuppositional faith will inevitably lead to wrong conclusions despite logic and the empirical evidence that proves otherwise.

It is important to note, though, that what alleged genetic studies do expose is that there is a correlation between close relationships and shared beliefs. It is not genes that cause or influence false beliefs and perspectives; rather, close relationships—especially familial relationships—promote like-minded beliefs and similar behavior.

Deception is not morally neutral and does not leave a person where it finds him/her. Just as people can increase in truth and understanding, they can also digress in their falsehood and arrive at a point of being so deceived that they are overwhelmed and controlled by it. The reality that one's faith and specifically deceit directly affects the physical nature explains why many people who are overwhelmed with deception have negatively altered and atrophied brains.[258] These observable symptoms do not indicate pathologies or etiologies of madness; they are simply the physical effects or manifestations of believing falsehood.

Today's biological psychiatrists insist that the body determines people's mental states and that the mind is a product of the brain. Thus, by accepting the philosophy of materialism, they must conclude that false fixed beliefs and perceptions (madness) are foundationally medical issues. Dr. Lieberman explains:

---

[257] Breggin, *Toxic Psychiatry*, 182-83.

[258] APA, *DSM-5*, 101-102.

> This declaration of the principles of biological psychiatry inspired a new contingent of psychiatric pioneers who believed that the key to mental illness did not lie within an ethereal soul or imperceptible magnetic channels but inside the soft, wet folds of tissue in the brain.[259]

As Lieberman correctly notes, the idea that the brain-dysfunction theory explains what causes someone to believe falsehood (madness) lacks valid empirical data. Furthermore, it is a belief that has not helped bring lucidity to the definition of madness; rather, it has confounded the concept and enabled its current fluidity and imprecision within psychiatric ideology.

Ironically, Emil Kraepelin, whom psychiatrists credit as establishing a truly biological/brain-based psychiatry, said of the "dominant brain-based approach" in the late 1800s, "Accordingly, it is at this point that fantasy, unfettered by the uncomfortable shackles of fact, begins to overtake the slow pace of empirical research."[260] Psychologist Engstrom and psychiatrist Kendler remark on Kraepelin's assertion,

> Kraepelin was deeply critical of the dominant brain-based approach to psychiatry led by the famous psychiatrist, neuro-anatomist, and chair of psychiatry in Vienna, Theodor Meynert (1833–1892). Kraepelin argued, in often pointed language, that the etiologic speculations of this school far outstripped the available findings.[261]

The brain-based theory of madness may very well be the greatest obstruction to psychiatrist's recognition and acceptance of the objective definition of madness observable throughout history.

A PROBLEM WITH BEHAVIOR

Without access to a person's mind, no one is able to determine whether another person is sane or mad. But as previously established, the mind is not accessible using scientific tools nor able to be studied through the scientific method. What

---

[259] Lieberman, *Shrinks*, 33.

[260] Kraepelin, *Psychiatrie*, 6th ed., 352.

[261] Engstrom and Kendler, "Emil Kraepelin: Icon and Reality," 1190-91.

has been universally and historically utilized in determining madness, though, is a person's observable behavior (including his/her audible words). By studying people's behavior and words, the essence of their soul can be somewhat discerned. But behavior is not a study of the soul nor the underlying problem; moral behaviors are only products of a person's mind, and these too can be carried out in deceit.

The German physician Wilhelm Wundt (who mentored both Sigmund Freud and Emil Kraepelin) was one of the first people to suggest using the scientific method in attempt to study the mind and its unhealthy thinking. Dr. Lieberman comments,

> Psychology (translated as "study of the soul") was a fledgling discipline that the German physician Wilhelm Wundt is credited with founding in 1879. Wundt was trained in anatomy and physiology, *but when the anatomical study of mental functions led to a dead end,* he turned to the outward manifestations of the brain reflected in human behavior and established an experimental laboratory devoted to behavior at the University of Leipzig.[262]

It was through Wundt, Kraepelin, and Freud that the study of behavior became seen as equaling the study of the soul, and thus, biological psychology and psychiatry were officially conceived. Behavioral psychologists today still suggest that they are studying the human psyche, but in truth they are only able to study behavior (including words) and observable human tendencies and patterns within a scientific framework.

The debate over defining madness is about not just whether someone's thinking is false or unhealthy, but also how to interpret a person's behavior. While the mind cannot be observed or measured with scientific tools, behaviors—physical manifestations of thoughts—are posited and classified as symptoms of mental illness within modern paradigms of madness. In large part, the various types, frequency, and duration of behaviors determine how madness is both recognized and categorized within the *DSM-5*. Following this modern psychiatric line of reason, one must conclude that

---

[262] Ibid., 64-65.

different behaviors with different durations constitute different types of mental illness. Likewise, such a theory proposes that types and duration of behaviors draw distinctions between normal and abnormal.

Some respected clinicians, however, do not believe that types of behavior differentiate madness from normalcy. Instead, figures such as well-respected psychologist Jerome Kagan assert that what causes behavior determines whether someone is normal or mad/mentally ill:

> Of course there are people who suffer from schizophrenia, who hear their great-grandfather's voice, for example, or who believe the Russians are shooting laser beams into their eyes. These are mentally ill people who need help. A person who buys two cars in a single day and the next day is unable to get out of bed has a bipolar disorder. And someone who cannot eat a bite in a restaurant because strangers could be watching them has a social phobia. There are people who, either for prenatal or inherited reasons, have serious vulnerabilities in their central nervous system that predispose them to schizophrenia, bipolar disease, social anxiety or obsessive-compulsive disorders. We should distinguish these people from all the others who are anxious or depressed because of poverty, rejection, loss or failure. *The symptoms may look similar, but the causes are completely different* [emphasis added].[263]

To date, there is no scientific evidence available to prove that false beliefs or false perceptions are caused by physical predispositions or biological causes.

The Diagnosis

Throughout history, observing a person's behavior has been the only consistent scientific means of identifying madness. Schizophrenia (Kraepelin's original construct of mental illness), for example, was created out of necessity to explain observable maladaptive thoughts and behavior, as Mary Boyle reveals,

> Schizophrenia, surely, was introduced and accepted because it was a reasonable (if imperfect) way of thinking about bizarre behaviour. It

---

263 Jerome Kagan, "What about Tutoring Instead of Pills?" *Spiegel Online*, August 2, 2012, http://www.spiegel.de/international/world/child-psychologist-jerome-kagan-on-overprescibing-drugs-to-children-a-847500.html.

> emerged because [Emil] Kraepelin 'discovered' it; it emerged as the result of a gradual process of more scientific, enlightened and humane treatment of the 'mentally ill.'[264]

Despite Boyle's claims, Kraepelin did not discover a type of madness or the concept that people have false fixed beliefs that can be deeply impairing and destructive; he simply formed a construct to explain these human tendencies and created a label to interpret common human behavior that was in his and many others' opinion otherwise unexplainable. As with Wundt and Kraepelin, Sigmund Freud relied on the same diagnostic tool of observing and categorizing patterns of common but undesirable behavior:

> Freud himself acknowledged general patterns of dysfunctional behavior—like hysteria, obsessiveness, phobias, anxiety, depression—but he believed they were all mutable manifestations of neuroses that grew out of emotional stresses occurring at specific stages of development.[265]

Freud understood that various behaviors represented different manifestations of madness rather than different types of madness, but his interpretation was entirely speculative. Despite Freud's and Kraepelin's opposing theories of insanity, they both relied entirely on what could be physically observed in order to classify and diagnose what they perceived to be mental disorder. They had not discovered any new diseases or even understood behavior to be a disease. Instead, they simply created their own construct, according to their own anthropology, in attempt to explain why someone's mind could be deceived enough to produce clear and measurable maladaptive behavior.

Like those before them, today's clinicians possess only a person's behavior—which they classify and list as symptoms—on which to base their diagnoses. Renowned Harvard psychologist Jerome Kagan remarks, "Psychiatry is the only medical profession in which the illnesses are only based on

---

264 Boyle, *Schizophrenia*, 17.

265 Lieberman, *Shrinks*, 96.

symptoms."[266] Psychiatrist Lawrie Reznek also acknowledges that "the ultimate test of whether we have accurately understood what someone believes lies with explaining that person's behavior."[267] Behaviors are vital in recognizing false beliefs, but contrary to modern psychiatric thinking, behaviors are not the key components in defining it, and behaviors do not provide a true or thorough look into the human soul.

While behavior may be the only viable tool to identify unhealthy thought processes, attempting to treat behavior (symptoms) does not resolve madness. Kagan explains with an enlightening illustration:

> There's a place in a large city with very bad drinking water, and kids are always getting sick with dysentery. So you keep treating the dysentery, but meanwhile it would be much better to clean up the drinking water.... The drugs work on the dysentery for about 48 hours, but you're not treating the problem. And the problem is not genetic.[268]

Observable behaviors are the effects of mental states and not the true substance. Not surprising, then, psychiatric and medical attempts which focus on behavior have throughout history failed to change anyone's faith from falsehood to truth, and psychotropic drugs which allegedly "change the psyche/soul" in a beneficial way do not truly exist.

Additionally, being able to suppress, restrain, or temporarily change maladaptive behavior with chemicals or physical restraints does not validate behavior as a physical disease or bring clarity to defining madness. The fact that psychoactive substances can and do restrain or alter behavior is not indication that behavior constitutes madness or that it is biologically caused. Placing someone in a straightjacket, for example, will also suppress behavior, but such a practice does not prove a deficiency of straightjacket use just as chemical restraints do not

---

266 Pettus, "Psychiatry by Prescription."

267 Reznek, *Delusions and Madness of the Masses*, 20.

268 Pettus, "Psychiatry by Prescription."

prove a deficiency or imbalance of chemicals. Despite the reality that addressing behavior (physical symptoms) through material means does not prove a biological etiology, the claim that mental illness is biologically caused is regularly made upon this premise.

The Interpretation

One of the principle reasons that many theories and definitions of madness now exist is that behaviors must be interpreted. If three people see a child climbing a bookshelf, for example, each will objectively observe the behavior but must subjectively interpret what they see. This interpretation will always reflect an underlying belief system. In other words, to interpret behavior and to figure out its executive control requires a presuppositional framework on the part of the observer. The APA recognizes in the *DSM-5* that different cultures interpret behaviors differently:

> Symptoms or behaviors that might be sorted by *DSM-5* into several disorders may be included in a single folk concept, and diverse presentations that might be classified by *DSM-5* as variants of a single disorder may be sorted into several distinct concepts by an indigenous diagnostic system. . . . Like culture and [the] *DSM* itself, cultural concepts may change over time in response to both local and global influences.[269]

Symptoms (behaviors) can be and are interpreted differently, which is why so many theories have existed in the last two centuries. When behavior becomes the focus of madness, instead of understanding that moral behavior is merely a manifestation of one's thinking, various interpretations of behavior will enable various definitions and constructs of madness to exist.

Although behaviors are observable, they are not objective means to define mental illness, since they are never interpreted apart from a person's faith. Psychiatrist Ed Shorter—highly regarded as a historian of biological psychiatry and madness—

---

[269] APA, *DSM-5*, 758.

relates how these "invisible diseases of the mind" (ones without biological markers or etiologies) require faith to accept:

> Research in psychiatry was part of a larger nineteenth-century current toward research in medicine in general. Doctors began to apply the clinical-pathological method: reasoning back and forth from findings at autopsy to the signs and symptoms the patient displayed before death. . . . Psychiatry in the nineteenth century too tried to attempt this clinical-pathological method, hoping to demonstrate the correctness of the biological approach rather than merely accept it on faith.[270]

While symptoms or behaviors are real, observable, and classifiable, how behaviors are interpreted is always in accordance with one's worldview. This fact requires faith both to discern another's thoughts and to interpret his/her behavior,[271] and the requirement of faith opens the door for beliefs about behavior to be false. Stated differently, theories of mental illness dogmatically held and based upon false interpretations of behavior can be delusions themselves.

By categorizing unhealthy mindsets and destructive behaviors into constructs of madness—creating a book of nosology—and asserting madness to be biological in nature, the APA has convinced many people to believe its formalized (yet fluid) interpretation of behavior found in the *DSM-5*. Former Professor of Psychiatry at Johns Hopkins University, psychiatrist Jerome Frank states:

> Ironically, mental health education, which aims to *teach people* how to cope more effectively with life, has instead increased the demand for psychotherapeutic help. *By calling attention to symptoms [behavior] they might otherwise ignore and by labeling those symptoms as signs of neurosis,* mental health education can create unwarranted anxieties, leading those to seek psychotherapy who do not need it [emphasis added].[272]

As Frank recognizes, "mental health education" often amounts to teaching people how to interpret behavior according to the

---

270 Shorter, *A History of Psychiatry*, 70.

271 Kagan, "Tutoring Instead of Pills?"

272 Jerome Frank, *Persuasion and Healing: A Comparative Study of Psychotherapy*, 1st ed. (Baltimore: Johns Hopkins University Press, 1961), 8.

APA's current formalized belief system. In an article published in 2017 in the *Psychiatric Times*, a committee at the *Group for the Advancement of Psychiatry* acknowledges this historical reality:

> The committee embarked upon a whirlwind tour of psychiatry, from ancient times through the present. In the process, Committee members made some eye-opening discoveries about health and illness over time and across cultures and continents. It was amazing to see that cultures around the world struggled with the same issues psychiatrists do today: *understanding mental suffering and behavioral differences through the filter of shared beliefs and practices, and applying remedies in accordance with those beliefs* [emphasis added].[273]

Throughout history, every culture has interpreted false believes according to a shared belief system.

The common practice of identifying, categorizing, and interpreting behavior according to a worldview, though, is not a medical endeavor; it is only considered a medical endeavor if the established worldview insists that behaviors be interpreted as medical issues. In fact, most of the constructs of mental illness listed in the *DSM-5* do not require any medical training or knowledge of human anatomy to recognize/diagnose. Instead, a person only needs to learn a categorization and system of interpreting behavior to diagnose *DSM-5* disorders. This reality explains, for example, why teachers are quick to identify children with behavioral problems in school as having ADHD. Instead of being valid medical issues, the *DSM-5* disorders are merely interpretations of behavior, and the *DSM-5*, itself, is not a scientific book about madness; rather, the *DSM-5* is one published belief about common impairing behavior that is born out of Darwinian evolutionary theory.[274]

Because the *DSM-5* describes specific relatable behavior, claims to be scientific and objective, and enjoys wide approval by the psychiatric industry, much of society has come to believe the APA's interpretation of their behavior; they are thinking and

---

273 Weiss and the *Group for the Advancement of Psychiatry*, "History of Psychiatry."

274 Porter, *Madness*, 183.

behaving as described in the *DSM-5*'s constructs. Labeling and categorizing seemingly odd, impairing, and undesirable behavior, though, does not legitimize a psychiatric construct; it simply represents one interpretation of behavior based upon a specific system of faith.

Furthermore, people must either interpret mindsets and behaviors according to either a dualistic or a materialistic worldview. Either moral behaviors reveal one's true nature or they are amoral. The Bible admonishes humanity to use moral behavior as an indicator of character, whereas the APA suggests that bad and impairing behavior exposes a disease. Despite their differences, both paradigms recognize behavior as historical and fundamental to identifying false fixed beliefs which are impairing and destructive.

CONCLUSION

Throughout history, madness has been a person's acceptance of false beliefs or a denial of truth/reality, and this mental state has been widely recognized as unhealthy, impairing, and destructive. Since the mind and its thoughts are immaterial and invisible, however, recognizing or diagnosing this destructive mental state occurs only by observing people's behavior and listening to their words (what the APA calls "symptoms").

While odd and dangerous behavior may be easy to recognize, discerning how to interpret such common behavior remains difficult for many and a contentious issue. In fact, the necessity to interpret people's maladaptive behavior according to one's moral system/worldview has yielded numerous opposing paradigms throughout history and across societies.

Psychiatry—once known as a custodial social service—is now thought of as medical and scientific field. In large part, their acceptance as physicians who care for the soul is due to the acceptance of their belief that all maladaptive mindsets and behaviors are biologically caused and thus medical issues. Through this new medical model of interpreting cognition and behavior, psychiatrists eventually gained authority, formed the APA, and published their ever-changing-formal standard of interpreting behavior: the *DSM*.

Despite the many claims over the last several decades, there exists no empirical evidence to conclude that the soul or its outworking behaviors are medical issues. Mental problems can certainly create health problems, but these struggles are not foundationally biologically caused. In contrast to the medical field of neurology that studies and treats the nervous system, psychiatry exists as an attempt to treat the false beliefs and mental frailty of humanity apart from God and His Word; it is a moral system which interprets behavior through materialism.

When the APA rejected Freud's interpretation of behavior and theory of the mind in the late 1940s and early 1950s, it quickly accepted Kraepelin's construct of mental illness as the standard of interpreting mindsets and behavior. This failed moral system, though, still lacks evidence to validate its theory of the mind or its interpretation of thoughts and behavior.

Madness is recognizable by observing a person's behavior, but behavior does not define mental illness, and seeking to primarily treat behaviors will never genuinely remedy the deceived mind. Simply because an alleged treatment suppresses or diminishes behavior does not mean that a cause or a remedy to madness has been found. Yet many in today's society have falsely come to believe that poor or impairing behavior defines mental illness and that mechanisms that suppress or diminish bad behavior constitute valid remedies.

CHAPTER 5

CONTROLLING MADNESS

"'The greatest sources of our suffering . . . are the lies we tell ourselves.'"[275]
Elvin Semrad, Professor of Psychiatry at Harvard University

"Men have called me mad; but the question is not yet settled, whether madness is or is not the loftiest intelligence– whether much that is glorious– whether all that is profound– does not spring from disease of thought– from moods of mind exalted at the expense of the general intellect. They who dream by day are cognizant of many things which escape those who dream only by night."[276]
Edgar Allen Poe, from "Elenora"

As discovered in the previous chapters, madness has historically been and remains defined as false fixed beliefs which are invisible and lack a known physical cause. However, determining falsehood always requires the establishment of objective truth. Therefore, in order to define and discuss madness, one must first determine what is true about human nature and specifically about the human mind. It cannot be overstated that the prevailing concept of truth will inevitably control definitions of mental illness.

Most modern theorists insist upon science being the determiner of what is true, and though the scientific method is

---

[275] Quoted by van der Kolk, *Body Keeps the Score,* 26-27.

[276] Edgar Allan Poe from "Eleonora," quoted in Neel Burton, *Psychiatry* 2nd ed. (West Sussex, UK: John Wiley and Sons, 2010), 97.

important in evaluating and discovering what is true in the physical world, what is true in the soul/psyche is not measurable with scientific methods. Instead, these truths—which determine what constitute false beliefs—are based upon the presuppositional faith of those who judge others to be mad. Truths that exist though they are unseen must be believed or rejected based on faith.

THE NECESSITY OF TRUTH

Madness—false beliefs and perceptions—cannot be defined, determined, or diagnosed unless essential truth is first established; deviances cannot exist without a clearly defined standard. Likewise, unless truth is objective and fixed, objective definitions of mental illness cannot logically exist or be imposed upon others.

Every definition of madness—whether dogmatically asserted or imprecisely suggested—always reflects a person's or society's beliefs about human nature's reality and what they believe to be true. Psychiatrist Lawrie Reznek contends,

> We cannot define a delusion without reference to the truth. If we define a delusion in terms of a conviction held in the face of obvious evidence to the contrary (the Incorrigibility Axiom), we are necessarily committed to some definition of delusions in terms of truth. This is because there is a conceptual connection between evidence and truth.[277]

The necessity to possess truth in order to define and evaluate madness is undeniable.

It cannot be said conversely, however, that constructs of mental illness establish what is true. Asserting objective definitions of madness—even claiming them as scientifically sound—without identifying the truth from which they originate is a logical fallacy. In fact, claiming to be an expert or authority in diagnosing madness assumes that a person possesses or is

---

[277] Reznek, *Delusions and Madness of the Masses,* preface xviii.

well-acquainted with truth. Professor of Clinical Psychiatry Sean Spence remarks,

> Why might deception be of interest to a clinical readership? Is it not a moral issue, more relevant to legal or theological discourse? . . . In psychiatry, neurology, medicolegal practice and perhaps certain other areas of medicine, doctors are called upon to judge the veracity of their patient's account (even though this may not be made explicit). Doctors commonly imply veracity in the terms that they use.[278]

Attempting to define madness by first categorizing and asserting theories of mental illness while at the same time ignoring or denying truths about human nature (normalcy) will inevitably fail. Working backwards while claiming normalcy does not exist objectively does not just fail: it is itself a fallacy and thus impairing.

The more difficult a truth is to accept, the greater the deception must be to deny it. When truth seemingly cannot be rationalized, understood, or resolved within our worldview, yet we are unwilling to alter our view of the world, then embracing deception is the only alternative. The key to understanding madness, then, is that it fundamentally explains people's poor relationship to truth/reality.

THE NATURE OF TRUTH

Although it is imperative to establish what is true about human nature and the mind in order to determine what is false, it is more important that the nature of truth be established first. If the nature of truth is not objective, then neither is falsehood. Consequently, if mental illness cannot be objectively defined, it does not logically exist; it is, then, insanity to diagnose people as being deceived or mad while at the same time insisting that truth is subjective.

---

[278] Spence, "Deceptive Brain," 6–9.

Similarly, to insist that definitions and constructs of abnormalities are objective without admitting or identifying the objective truth foundational to their existence is absurd and misleading. If truth is relative, so too is madness, and such a reality determines the APA's claim that the *DSM-5* and their many suggested disorders are empirically sound (objective) to be itself a delusion.

In considering the nature of truth, there exists two common but opposing theories: people either believe that (1) truth is relevant, evolving, and determined by community consensus, or that (2) truth is external, fixed, and objective.

Most secular theorists of mental illness insist that truth is relevant and ever changing; thus, in their estimation mental illness cannot be defined with precision or reliability. The *DSM* begins with this disclaimer:

> While *DSM* has been the cornerstone of substantial progress in reliability, it has been well recognized by both the American Psychiatric Association (APA) and the broad scientific community working on mental disorders that past science was not mature enough to yield fully validated diagnoses—that is, to provide consistent, strong, and objective scientific validators of individual *DSM* disorders. The science of mental disorders continues to evolve. . . . Speculative results do not belong in an official nosology, but at the same time, *DSM* must evolve in the context of other clinical research initiatives in the field.[279]

The APA's perspective on truth represents the Aristotelian tradition, which minimized universal/objective truth and focused instead on relative abstract disease concepts that might manifest differently. German philosopher and atheist Friedrich Nietzsche held to this philosophy and insisted that "there are no facts, only interpretations."[280] The APA shares this same belief, and it asserts that the alleged diseases of the mind found in the *DSM-5* are not objective and are ever-changing. In contrast to the Aristotelian view,

---

279 APA, *DSM-5*, 5.

280 Friedrich Nietzsche, *The Portable Nietzsche*, ed. and trans. Walter Kaufmann (London: Penguin Books, 1977), 458.

> the platonic tradition taught that reality was universal and unchanging, unlike perceptions received through the senses, which were relative and imperfect. Applied to medicine, these ideas led to a search for unvarying universals—individual diseases 'out there' and separable from the person.[281]

What is claimed to be true within Aristotelian thinking is speculative scientism that is constantly changing—especially as applied to the Kraepelinian theory of mental illness. This faulty ideology governs modern psychiatric ideas of mental illness and permits what is judged to be empirically sound and true today to be exposed as a delusion tomorrow.

The field of psychiatry itself was formed on the failed "science" of phrenology (1790-1820)—"a science of character divination,"[282] the speculative belief that "the brain is the seat of the mind," and that "mental facilities have specific anatomical locations."[283] The *Group for the Advancement of Psychiatry* explains how psychiatry was conceived: "Though a flawed science that gave way to fantism[[284]], phrenology, we could say, was the midwife to modern psychiatry."[285] Built on "flawed science" ("the science of the mind"[286]) modern psychiatrists still hope that "as the biomedical model increases our knowledge of serious mental disorders, it will eventually destroy the myth we have held in the meantime."[287] Alleged "science[s] of human

---

[281] Boyle, *Schizophrenia*, 8.

[282] John van Wyhe, "The History of Phrenology on the Web," http://www.historyofphrenology.org.uk/overview.htm.

[283] Group for the Advancement of Psychiatry, "The History of Psychiatry 19th Century," 3:52-5:14.

[284] *Fantism* is an antiquated belief system or ideology that persists with passionate supporters who discuss it at length but cannot agree upon what it actually is or means.

[285] Group for the Advancement of Psychiatry, "The History of Psychiatry 19th Century," 3:52-5:14.

[286] Wyhe, "History of Phrenology."

[287] Watters and Ofshe, *Therapy's Delusions*, 27.

nature"[288]—as they relate to the incorporeal aspects of mankind—are not valid sciences.

Sigmund Freud's construct of mental illness (psychoanalysis) provides one example of how psychiatric theories of human nature can easily change from being accepted as dogma by psychiatrists and much of society to being viewed as delusions. Sociologists Ethan Watters and Richard Ofshe remark,

> In providing a language with which we could describe and seem to explain our behavior, the idea of the psychodynamic mind occupied a void in our increasingly science-based culture that religion had once filled. The unique qualities of the human mind and human feeling that were once simply assumed to be God-given were accounted for by Freud and his followers through an amalgam of simplistic evolutionary biology and theories about unconscious impulses. Accepted in America as profound truths, these assumptions about the mind and behavior were incorporated in the middle of the century into university teachings and found wide reception in popular culture. Several generations of psychologists and psychiatrists built their careers on these premises.[289]

Watters and Ofshe later state about these once-accepted "profound truths":

> Freud created one of the twentieth century's most significant myths but presented it as a scientific theory, supposedly based on rationalism and empirical observation. He claimed to be opening up the complexity of the mind to the world, but in fact he created a convoluted and speculative system of assumptions that has misled thousands upon thousands of well-intentioned therapists and vulnerable patients over the last hundred years.[290]

It is important to note that for decades the APA believed Freudianism with unwavering conviction, and to believe otherwise was considered by psychiatrists at that time to be taboo and even delusional. Former APA president Jeffrey Lieberman expounds on this history,

> By 1960, almost every major psychiatry position in the country was occupied by a psychoanalyst. There were twenty psychoanalytic

---

288 Wyhe, "History of Phrenology."

289 Ibid., 22-23.

290 Ibid., 16.

> training institutes across the United States, many affiliated with psychiatry departments at top universities. . . . By then [1960], virtually all clinical psychiatrists—whether formally credentialed or not—were psychoanalytically oriented. In 1924, the first Freud-leaning psychiatrist was elected president of the APA, and the next fifty-eight years witnessed an almost unbroken series of psychoanalyst presidents of the American Psychiatric Association.[291]

Lieberman also recognizes how delusional the APA was to believe in the Freudian theory of mental illness—even suggesting that a diagnosis of mania described its own mental state:

> By 1955, a majority of psychoanalysists had concluded that all forms of mental illness—including neuroses and psychoses—were manifestations of inner psychological conflicts. But the hubris of the American psychoanalytic movement didn't stop there. At this point, if it had been able to lie upon its own therapeutic couch, the *psychoanalytic movement would have been diagnosed with all the classic symptoms of mania: extravagant behaviors, grandiose beliefs, and irrational faith in its world-changing powers* [emphasis added].[292]

But what if today's accepted neo-Kraepelinian theory—like Freud's before him—is realized to be false? What if neo-Kraepelinians, who claim that their theory is scientific and rational, are just as delusional as Freudians? Psychiatrist Sir Robin Murray, for decades regarded by most of his peers and throughout the medical profession as the premier researcher on the construct of schizophrenia, changed his dogmatic belief in Kraepelinianism. In an article published in the *Schizophrenia Bulletin* at the end of 2016, he proclaimed that fellow psychiatrists should now consider Kraepelinianism to be a delusion:

> Amazingly, such is the power of the Kraepelinian model that some psychiatrists still refuse to accept the evidence, and cling to the nihilistic view that there exists an intrinsically progressive

---

291 Lieberman, *Shrinks*, 75.

292 Ibid., 83.

> schizophrenic process, a view greatly to the detriment of their patients.[293]

In the same article, Dr. Murray concedes that he can no longer support the construct of schizophrenia—which Kraepelin created—as a valid biological illness.[294] Others have written books, such as Mary Boyle's *Schizophrenia: A Scientific Delusion,*[295] which systematically present empirical evidence that exposes the notion of schizophrenia and psychosis being biological illnesses to be a delusion. After careful scientific research led him to conclude that psychiatrists embrace false fixed beliefs (that hurt people rather than help them) despite clear evidence to the contrary, Danish physician, medical researcher, and leader of the Nordic Cochrane Research Center wrote a book entitled, *Deadly Psychiatry and Organised Denial.*[296] Considered at the turn of the century to be "perhaps the most powerful psychiatrist in America,"[297] Allen Francis also asserts about psychiatry's alleged science of mental illness: "What seem now to be fanciful myths were once the best science of the time, and our current best science will itself in the not-too-distant future be seen as no more than fanciful myth."[298]

Is it possible that those who hold to the modern neo-Kraepelinian theory of genetics (eugenics), brain dysfunction, and chemical imbalances are actually delusional and simply do not recognize it yet? Watters and Ofshe expect future discovery to unveil this exact scenario: "As the biomedical model increases

---

[293] Murray, "Mistakes I Have Made in My Research Career."

[294] Ibid.

[295] Mary Boyle, *Schizophrenia: A Scientific Delusion?* 2nd ed. (London: Routledge, 2002).

[296] Peter C. Gotzsche, *Deadly Psychiatry and Organised Denial* (ArtPeople, 2015), Kindle. Loc 164.

[297] Greenberg, *Book of Woe,* 22.

[298] Frances, *Saving Normal,* 36.

our knowledge of serious mental disorders, it will eventually destroy the myth we have held in the meantime."[299] Continuing to believe falsehood and denying reality is madness, and those who continue believing Kraepelinian theory despite the clear impairment and destruction it has brought on individuals and society since its conception must deny empirical evidence in order to sustain their false theory.

When delusions become the social norm, then society is put in a far more dangerous position then when it is faced with only an individual's false beliefs. Carl Jung cautions that

> the ordinary lunatic is generally a harmless, isolated case; since everyone sees that something is wrong with him, he is quickly taken care of. But the unconscious infections of groups of so-called normal people are more subtle and far more dangerous.[300]

If Kraepelinianism is a false fixed belief system, then the APA as a whole has once again become mad, and accepting these delusions places society in the same dangerous position as it did when the APA dogmatically believed Freudianism to be true.

This reality is the direct result of following Aristotelian thinking, which permits delusions to be claimed as objective truth while simultaneously claiming truth to be imprecise. This practice, of course, is fallacious; if truth is relative and constantly changing, then delusions become the inescapable norm and objective truth can never exist. Madness too, then, would forever be a subjective concept; a never-ending cycle of falsehood—first claimed to be truth and then shown to be false—would characterize all scientific endeavors and attempts to define mental illness. Following such logic makes insanity normative, and adhering to this way of thinking is enough to drive anyone mad.

Clearly, delusions cannot be objectively determined unless truth is first objectively and immutably defined. To believe

---

[299] Watters and Ofshe, *Therapy's Delusions*, 27.

[300] Carl G. Jung, *The Integration of the Personality*, trans. Stanley Dell (New York: Farrar & Rinehart Inc., 1939), 9.

otherwise is to accept the perspective of American film director and producer Tim Burton, who once said, "One person's craziness is another person's reality."[301] If truth is relative and not fixed, so too is insanity. The current psychiatric system of mental health—which is used to dogmatically diagnose people as being abnormal or disordered, then, is itself madness.

THE BENEFIT OF ABSOLUTE TRUTH

Another problem in claiming truth to be relative is that anyone's idea of truth can be asserted to define and ultimately diagnose others as mad. Those who are given the greatest authority will be entitled to establish their standard of truth—even if their standard is not actually truth. If people are morally sound, then their standard of truth can be beneficial. But if an authority is evil, has a selfish agenda, or is deceived, then ideas of what constitutes truth and human nature can be destructive and even horrific when carried out to their practical end. Accepting fixed moral truth apart from one's own false beliefs enables individuals and society to be altruistic and prosper and protects them from much evil. Conversely, without objective truth, chaos will inevitably ensue, and concepts of mental illness—based on false presumptions—will be used as societal control mechanisms.

A cursory overview of madness throughout history reveals that defining and controlling ideas of madness (what is true and what is false) have indisputably been powerful societal control mechanisms. Take for an example the time during the Reformation and Counter-Reformation. The secular historian Roy Porter observes,

> In the conflagration of heresy—accusations and burnings stoked by the Reformation and Counter-Reformation, false doctrine and delusion formed two sides of the same coin: the mad were judged to be

---

301 Tim Burton, quoted by Eiss, *Insanity and Genius*, 599.

possessed, and religious adversaries were deemed out of their mind.[302]

Several hundred years later in the 1860s, Calvinist pastor Reverend Packard had his wife Elizabeth Packard committed to the Jacksonville Insane Asylum in Illinois for holding to beliefs which differed from the creed of the Presbyterian church.[303] Mrs. Packard was diagnosed as insane by physicians and held for three years against her will simply because she held to beliefs which were contrary to those of the established clerical authority. This practice has occurred with ease throughout history, since as Porter notes, there exists no valid distinction between delusions and false doctrines; both are considered to be false fixed beliefs.

In addition, consider one of the most prominent examples: The Holocaust. The Jews were labeled as mentally ill by the father of the modern secular construct of mental illness, psychiatry, and psychopharmacology, Emil Kraepelin.[304] Kraepelin's definition of madness, coupled with Germany's utilitarian application, would bring about the Holocaust under the direction of Kraepelin's premier student, Ernst Rüdin. Psychiatrist Peter Breggin notes,

> When Hitler came to power, Rüdin was ready for him. It was Rüdin who influenced Hitler, not Hitler who influenced Rüdin. The psychiatrist became the architect and official interpreter of the first legislation establishing the Nazi eugenics program that lead to the castration and sterilization of tens of thousands of individuals accused of being schizophrenic, retarded, epileptic, or in some other way physically or mentally "defective." . . . Rüdin's mountainous publications on genetics, pivotal under German rule during World War II, stimulated acceptance of the eventual slaughter of the Jews as well.[305]

---

302 Porter, *Madness*, 21.

303 Group for the Advancement of Psychiatry, "The History of Psychiatry 19th Century."

304 Berger, *Necessity for Faith and Authority*, 63-71.

305 Breggin, *Toxic Psychiatry*, 102.

Clinical psychologist Richard Bentall also comments,

> In the following years, Nazi policies were gradually embraced by the German psychiatric establishment, championed in particular by Ernst Rüdin, who had been recruited to the Institute by Kraepelin in order to develop the new field of psychiatric genetics. The eugenic theories that Rüdin proposed led, first, to the enforced sterilization and then, later, the killing of mentally ill patients.[306]

Belief in utilitarianism enabled both the acceptance of Kraepelin's construct of madness and eugenics within German society as well as its horrific application. Dr. Allen Frances maintains that

> there are also undeniable uncertainties in being a practical utilitarian, and even worse there are *dangerous value land mines.* "The greatest good for the greatest number" sounds great on paper, but how do you measure the quantities and *how do you decide what's the good?* It is no accident that utilitarianism is currently least popular in Germany, where Hitler gave it such an enduringly bad name. During World War II, it was statistically normal for the German population to act in barbaric ways that would be deemed decidedly abnormal before or since—all justified at the time on utilitarian grounds as necessary to provide for the greatest good of the master race [emphasis added].[307]

Historian Andrew Scull reveals how prominent genetic theories (still regularly asserted as fact) attached to the concept of madness brought about the Holocaust:

> Hitler's Germany took such notions to their logical conclusion: with the active and enthusiastic participation of many German psychiatrists, mental patients were sent in their thousands to the gas ovens. (More than 70,000 were gassed in just 20 months, beginning in January 1940.)[308]

Psychiatrists Andreas Ebert and Karl-Jürgen Bär wrote in the *Indian Journal of Psychiatry* about Kraepelin and his ideas of madness:

> One of the most problematical issues about Kraepelin is his generalization of psychiatric findings to social and political contexts.

---

306 Bentall, *Madness Explained,* 30.

307 Frances, *Saving Normal,* 5.

308 Scull, *Madness,* 6.

> For example, socialists and opponents of World War I were judged to be mentally ill by him. *He also theorized about frequent genetic predispositions for psychiatric disorders in Jews* [emphasis added].[309]

Nazi eugenics and Kraepelin's construct of mental illness were themselves delusions, yet practically an entire nation accepted them as true. If truth is relative and a person's beliefs do not match your own, then given enough power, you can judge others to be mad.

But some psychiatrists, such as Lawrie Reznek, recognize a serious problem with believing that truth is relative:

> There seems to be a deep problem here. If what is regarded as reality varies from society to society, then who is judged as sane will vary from social perspective to social perspective. In this view, any single society will have a set of truths that makes up this social reality, and a class of socially sanctioned reasons to believe such truths. If someone in that society holds different beliefs and defends them vehemently, then *ipso facto* he is deluded. . . . Madness seems to be a relative matter. Paranoia is in the eye of the beholder.[310]

Madness is a relative matter only if truth is too. If truth about human nature is ever-changing, subjective, and dependent upon popular opinion, then people can use constructs of madness for selfish and inhumane advantage, and individuals or specific groups can construct definitions of madness to advance their own beliefs or agendas. History reveals that labeling someone as mentally ill without morally establishing objective truth about human nature and sound faith is itself destructive and enables the concept of mental illness to be used as a social control mechanism.

THE ARRIVAL AT TRUTH

Those who diagnose or judge others to be mad or mentally ill must first insist that their own concept of truth be accepted and upheld in society. In other words, judging others to be mad

---

309 Ebert and Bär, "Emil Kraepelin," 191-92.

310 Reznek, *Delusions and Madness of the Masses*, 26.

presupposes that truth and authority about human nature and the mind/psyche have been objectively established and should be universally accepted. But how people determine what constitutes truth about human nature (what is normalcy) has been and remains a matter of contention and disagreement.

For madness to exist, value judgments or morals must also exist. Reznek maintains,

> Overall, then, we make the value judgment that in general we are better off being free of delusions. . . . Given our value judgment here, a delusion qualifies as a means whereby we can recognize mental illness.[311]

The common belief is that false beliefs are impairing and destructive—that they are bad—and accepting and promoting truth is good for people individually and corporately. A concept of truth and deception (good and bad) are a part of every disorder that psychiatrists construct. Still, many psychiatrists seek to eliminate the consideration of human morality by asserting their biological construct of madness. According to psychiatrist and co-founder of the World Federation of Mental Health Brock Chisholm, "If the race is to be freed from the crippling burden of good and evil, it must be psychiatrists who take the original responsibility."[312] But the fact that delusions and hallucinations are by nature considered to be false and falsehood to be viewed as bad reveals that a moral system is still in place.

The former president-elect of the APA Jeffery Lieberman acknowledges that the APA has (through the *DSM*) posited their concepts of human nature as objective truth to guide society's beliefs:

> Psychiatry has become deeply ingrained within the fabric of our culture, winding through our most prominent social institutions and coloring our most mundane daily encounters. For better or worse, the

---

311 Ibid., preface xxvi.

312 "Undermining Morals," Citizen's Commission on Human Rights UK, http://www.cchr.org.uk/psychiatric-drugs/undermining-morals/.

> *DSM* is not merely a compendium of medical diagnoses. *It has become a public document that helps define how we understand ourselves and how we live our lives* [emphasis added].[313]

This public document suggests a theory of what is true about human nature and specifically the human mind/psyche. But how did the APA arrive at their beliefs about what is true and what is madness?

The Humanistic Perspective

The APA along with other humanistic theorists insist both that the community must be the primary vehicle to deliver a society at truth's doorstep and that the community or majority is the only safe-guard against forming theories of truth which are destructive and barbaric. In fact, the APA has included in its definition of delusions a concept of community which, in their opinion, is vital to establishing truth and false beliefs. This concept is often referred to as the "community qualifier" or "community axiom."[314] The *DSM-5* defines delusions (false fixed beliefs) based upon "what almost everyone else believes."[315] It also says, "The belief is not ordinarily accepted by other members of the person's culture or subculture (i.e., it is not an article of religious faith)."[316] The psychiatric ideas of truth and madness depend greatly upon the majority's agreed upon beliefs.

The community axiom is the practical application of *utilitarianism*—the greatest good for the greatest number as decided by the greatest authority or the majority. Utilitarianism is the fundamental belief that guides psychiatrists' ever-changing imprecise definitions and many theories of madness.

---

313 Lieberman, *Shrinks*, 291.

314 Reznek, *Delusions and Madness of the Masses*, preface xviii.

315 APA, *DSM-5*, 819.

316 Ibid.

Ultimately, the social axiom of mental illness governs their ideas of human morality and their concepts of truth/normalcy. Dr. Allen Frances states,

> Utilitarianism provided the first, and remains the only practical, philosophical guidance on how and where to set a boundary between "normal" and "mental disorder." . . . Granted that, in the wrong hands, utilitarianism can be blind to good values and twisted by bad ones, it still remains the best or only philosophical guide when we embark on the difficult task of setting boundaries between the mentally "normal" and the mentally "abnormal." This is the approach we used in *DSM-IV*.[317]

Is adhering to the majority's opinion about truth which cannot be observed with scientific methods—especially truths concerning human nature and the mind—the best way to arrive at a guiding view of normalcy and madness? Frances is correct in admitting, however, that utilitarianism requires "good values" and is a "philosophical guide." In other words, utilitarianism can never replace morality in helping humanity to arrive at truth. Without right underlying moral faith, individuals will not accept truth or genuinely care about the welfare of others, and in the same way, without underlying moral faith, large groups will inevitably deny truth. Though utilitarianism does not replace the necessity of morality to guide beliefs, there are three primary reasons why the APA continues to insist upon the community qualifier to define delusions and thus mental illness.

Relativism

The first reason is that they are mostly relativists who believe that truth is subjective and ever-changing. That is, however, except when it comes to their currently endorsed and published concepts of madness (e.g., the current *DSM-5* disorders).

Each time the APA asserts a new definition of madness, it insists that its new imprecise construct be accepted by society as

---

[317] Frances, *Saving Normal*, 5.

scientific fact. The notion that truth is evolving enables the APA's conjecture to continue under the guise of scientific advancement. But if there are no absolute truths—only relativism, then no position at all is worthy of establishing, and the *DSM* becomes a subjective belief of no real value that society will eventually consider to be a delusion.

The problem with this position is that truth, by definition, requires immutability, reliability, and validity. Moreover, if truth is not objective and fixed, then neither is science, which largely depends upon precisely defined and claimed truth. As philosophers for centuries have been pointing out, if there are no absolute truths, then dogmatically claiming that there are no absolute truths and defending such a notion is a logical fallacy.

Furthermore, if truth is understood to be objective and not merely relevant to situations and people, then morality and eventually a deity must also be accepted. Instead of truth being conceptualized as internal and relative to the individual, truth will be discovered as externally fixed and universal. The concepts of relativism, utilitarianism, and materialism are moral beliefs which attempt to resolve the reality of human morality and the objective and external nature of truth.[318]

Normalcy

There is a second reason why the APA insists upon the community axiom—especially in religious settings: if entire communities are found to be delusional, then the diagnosis of disorder/abnormality/mental illness is cheapened. If large groups of people were at the same time diagnosed as being mentally ill or delusional, then madness would be viewed as an impairing aspect of normal human nature and not as an abnormality—something outside of the norm. The community axiom is vital to the psychiatric idea of mental illness not only to protect the belief that madness is a form of abnormality

---

[318] See Daniel R. Berger II, *Mental Illness: The Reality of the Spiritual Nature* (Taylors, SC: Alethia International Publications, 2016).

(something apart from the norm), a disorder, and a mental illness, but also to keep truth as an alleged product of community collaboration rather than as externally fixed and objective. The community axiom also protects the APA itself from being considered delusional based upon its past faith in Freudianism and its current belief in Kraepelinianism.

The community qualifier explains why psychiatrists do not formally judge religious people to be delusional, though many such as psychiatrist Lawrie Reznek believe that they are:

> Of all our beliefs, religious beliefs are the ones that we cling to more than any other belief. More than other belief systems, these are resistant to evidence to the contrary. When have you ever heard a religious person say: "You know, you're right: there is no God"? Rather, one is inclined to hear ad hoc hypothesis layered on ad hoc hypothesis as people cling to their religious beliefs.[319]

Furthermore, Reznek theorizes about the reason the APA has yet to proclaim Catholics and evangelicals, for example, as being mad:

> Not all convictions that are held come what may and that are likely false are classified as delusions. A Catholic is mistakenly convinced that when her priest performs Mass, an ordinary wafer and a glass of wine turn into the flesh and blood of Jesus Christ. But this is not considered to be a delusion because the belief is shared by members of her community (Community Axiom). Psychiatry assumes that this is not a delusion because a whole community subscribes to it. The Judaic-Christian belief that God created the world six thousand years ago in exactly six days is adhered to by many with convictions and is almost certainly false. But psychiatry doesn't classify this as a delusion. Because psychiatrists don't want to classify whole (religious) communities as deluded, they conclude the Community Axiom into the definition of a delusion.[320]

If large groups or the majority of people are delusional, according to the APA, these people should not be considered mad.

But there is a serious problem with attempting to allow society's opinion or the community axiom to determine what is

---

319 Reznek, *Delusions and Madness of the Masses*, 62.

320 Ibid., preface xviii.

true: large groups and entire societies can be and regularly are delusional. Atheist philosopher Friedrich Nietzsche explains, "In individuals, insanity is rare; but in groups, parties, nations and epochs, it is the rule."[321] As observed already in this chapter, the APA's shared false belief in Freudianism for decades provides an ironic example. But history is replete with other examples of whole communities who were deeply deceived in impairing and behaviorally destructive ways. It is no wonder that Voltaire once said, "Those who can make you believe absurdities can make you commit atrocities."[322]

If one person believes a lie to be true, it is likely that others will also believe and behave accordingly despite a belief's absurdity. Take for example, the historical account of David Koresh and the "Branch Davidian" cult that he founded. After convincing over eighty people to believe that he was the messiah, gaining their complete devotion, and moving them all into a compound outside Waco, Texas, Koresh did horrific things to his believers. The words and conduct of Koresh's followers were so outrageous the FBI concluded that the Branch Davidians "were not in their right minds."[323] Many psychiatrists diagnose Koresh and his followers in hind-sight to have been "mentally ill."[324] Soon after the bizarre behavior was discovered by the FBI, a conflict between government agents and the compound ensued, and after weeks of standoff passed, many members of the cult followed Koresh to their death. Despite how

---

321 Friedrich Nietzsche quoted by Eiss, *Insanity and Genius*, 599.

322 Voltaire, *Miracles and Idolatry*, trans. Theodore Besterman (London: Penguin, 2010 [first published in 1764]), Gale ECCO, electronic edition.

323 John Burnett, "After Two Decades, Some Branch Davidians Still Believe," *NPR Online*, April 20, 2013, http://www.npr.org/2013/04/20/178063471/two-decades-later-some-branch-davidians-still-believe.

324 Reznek, *Delusions and Madness of the Masses*, 82-84.

events unfolded and the death of their leader, many survivors of the cult still believe in David Koresh and await his return.[325]

What psychiatrics have failed to consider or address within their concept of truth is that education and faith function on the communal transference of proposed truth. In other words, faith—whether it is true and beneficial or false and impairing—is translated through close relationships and community thought. This fact is why psychotherapies or "talk therapies" can and regularly do influence a counselee's beliefs, and why siblings that endured traumatic experiences together share common false beliefs. Highly regarded by biological psychiatrists, Eric Kandel wrote in his book *Psychiatry, Psychoanalysis, and the New Biology of Mind* that

> Psychotherapy presumably works by creating an environment in which people learn to change. If those changes are maintained over time, it is reasonable to conclude that psychotherapy leads to structural changes in the brain, just as other forms of learning do. Indeed, we can already image people's brains before and after therapy and thus see the consequences of psychotherapeutic intervention in certain disorders.[326]

As a person's faith changes through relationships—for good or for bad—so too does the brain's structure.

But even the APA recognizes false faith can be shared between two or more people. The APA described this reality in the *DSM-IV* as *folie à deux* ("the madness of two") or "shared psychotic (delusional) disorder" and replaced it with "Delusional symptoms in partner of individual with delusional disorder" in the *DSM-5*[327]:

> In the context of a relationship, the delusional material from the dominant partner provides content for delusional belief by the

---

325 Burnett, "Some Branch Davidians Still Believe."

326 Eric Kandel, *Psychiatry, Psychoanalysis, and the New Biology of Mind* (Arlington, VA: American Psychiatric Publishing, 2005), 386.

327 The APA removed "shared psychotic disorder" from being published in the *DSM-5* as a formal disease. The APA, instead, placed the idea under the subtype of "Other Specified Schizophrenic Spectrum and Other Psychotic Disorders" (APA, *DSM-5*, 122).

individual who may not otherwise entirely meet criteria for delusional disorder.[328]

Other clinicians remark,

> Shared psychotic disorder or its more common synonym, *folie à deux*, is a rare clinical syndrome. Its characteristic feature is transmission of delusions from "inducer" (primary patient), who is the "originally" ill patient and suffers from a psychotic disorder, to another person who may share the inducer's delusions in entirety or in part. Depending on whether the delusions are shared among two, three, four, five and even twelve people, it is called as folie à deux, folie à trios, folie à quatre, folie à cinq and folie à douze. Shared psychotic disorder is mostly observed among people who live in close proximity and in close relationships. It is found in parent-offspring, sibling-sibling, or husband-wife constellations. Furthermore, mother-daughter or sister-sister pairs represents fifty percent of the psychotic dyads.[329]

Although shared beliefs may be posited as rare by psychiatrists, they are fundamental to most of society. When beliefs are negative or false, however, the APA suggests that beliefs are abnormalities or disorders. Such a notion assumes that so-called normal people are not easily deceived—especially large groups of people all at once.

Psychiatrist Lawrie Reznek comments on another cult similar to the Branch Davidians: Marshall Applewhite and the Heaven's Gate cult. He notes how delusional thinking typically starts with one person's ideas and then easily spreads within close relationships:

> Here we have a classic story of what I call *folie a culte*. Like *folie a deux*, it starts off with the mental illness of a dominant figure. Applewhite appeared to suffer from schizophrenia—a disorder characterized by delusions and hallucinations. He developed a close relationship with his nurse, Nettles, and she appears to have developed *folie* a *deux*. For a while, only the two of them shared Applewhite's madness. However, they then attracted followers who, like Nettles, were sucked into Applewhite's madness. All of the members of the Heaven's Gate cult came to acquire the delusional ideas of their leader. They came to believe that Applewhite was indeed an alien, and that by killing

---

328 Ibid.

329 Atefeh Ghanbari Jolfaei, Mehdi Nasr Isfahani, and Reza Bidaki, "Folie À Deux and Delusional Disorder by Proxy in a Family," *Journal of Research in Medical Sciences: Official Journal of Isfahan University of Medical Sciences* 16, no. 1 (2011): S453–S455.

> themselves, they would ascend to a level higher than human beings, join the spaceship hidden in the tail of Hale-Bopp and travel to the Kingdom of God. So convinced of these ideas were they that they all committed suicide on the delusional conviction that this was the "exit" they needed.[330]

Reznek goes on to point out that these historical cases undermine the psychiatric idea that society or the majority will arrive at truth and corporately avoid false fixed beliefs. The notion that humanity by nature tends to believe truth is undermined by reality. Whether the leader is David Koresh, Marshall Applewhite, Jim Jones, the head of the APA, or Adolf Hitler, community does not safeguard against delusions, and it is not a valid determiner of what is true and what is false.

What Reznek also acknowledges is that the APA's concept of madness must exclude the consideration that majorities or at least large multitudes can be so deceived as to be considered mad:

> Psychiatry makes assumptions about who is mad and who is not. On the one hand, psychiatrists assume that people (most of whom we call schizophrenics) are mad and suffering from delusions. On the other hand, psychiatrists assume that members of religious communities are not delusional, and that cultures are subcultures that entertain such deviant secular beliefs (such as the belief in the paranormal) are also not deluded. They then define the notion of delusion in such a way to differentiate these two groups of people. In this way, psychiatry simply begs the question. It starts off assuming what it hopes to prove. It wants to prove that religious communities are not deluded but has to start off assuming this.[331]

Thus, in order to view an issue or concept as true and not as a delusion, psychiatrists must assume that a community's acceptance and concurrence validates that matter to be true.

There is no logical basis not to consider that all of those who believed Applewhite's false teachings, for example, and eventually committed suicide were themselves not mad in the same way as Applewhite. Yet this understanding undermines

---

330 Reznek, *Delusions and Madness of the Masses*, 78.

331 Ibid., 72.

the "community's acceptance" tenet of the APA. Still, entire communities regularly share common false fixed beliefs:

> In the end, there is no good reason not to classify all the members of the Heaven's Gate cult as psychotic. . . . I think we can safely say having reviewed these examples of *folie a culte*, that whole communities can be deluded. A single person living in close proximity to a charismatic or dominant psychotic individual can become psychotic herself. This disorder is called *folie a deux*.[332]

In order to accept the APA's community acceptance clause people must believe that society or at least a large group always provides protection against falsehood. While the widespread acceptance of truth can be beneficial to a society, widespread acceptance of deception is destructive to both the individual and the group. Truth does not rest in the majority's opinion or in utilitarianism, and it is not relative. In other words, society does not determine what is true, but it too, as with each individual, must accept or reject objective truth.

Causation

There is a third reason that the APA must guard against considering madness as a social reality: the acceptance of false fixed beliefs (whether individually or corporately) and their corresponding behavior are regularly conceived within relationships and not in a person's biology (e.g., brain, genetics, or neurochemicals). Psychiatrist and historian Petteri Pietikäinen explains,

> As a historian I believe in situational explanations of behavior: the explanation for much of our behavior is linked to our social context. People live within the institutions and social structures that organize their lives. This includes parents, relatives, friends, members of the community, authority figures, religion, economy, educational institutions and the political system. *Prevailing cultural beliefs shape our world views and our self-understanding* [emphasis added].[333]

---

332 Ibid., 79; 86.

333 Pietikäinen, *Madness*, 7.

Close relationships and shared experiences encourage like-minded beliefs and behavior, yet the modern theorist attempts only to link impairing false beliefs to speculative genetic causes. Dr. Peter Breggin comments,

> Families share political outlooks, national feelings, cultural values and prejudices and languages; but nowadays scientists do not consider these traits to be genetic in origin.[334]

But true and false beliefs are widely understood to be learned and accepted within the family. For example, *Medscape Psychiatry* published an article in 2016 in which the authors exposed how delusions are common among siblings and parents:

> Soriano *et al* presented a case of *folie à deux* that occurred between 2 sisters. As in the parent-child relationship, the occurrence of shared psychotic delusions among siblings is common due to the close ties. As the authors of this study discussed with regard to the sisters, the occurrence among siblings can be particularly attributed to shared past experience or expectations.[335]

In the case of Marshall Applewhite, delusions were clearly not spread through genetics but through social interaction. This reality undermines materialists' assertion that mental illness is a medical or genetic issue, and it, in part, also explains why the medical model has failed miserably over the last sixty years to correct people's false beliefs and false perceptions.

The Biblical Perspective

In contrast to the secular explanations for truth and human nature, the Bible's explanations are much simpler, clearer, and less fluid. The Bible begins with the simple premise that the universe was a purposeful creation of an all wise God. If such a God did indeed create the universe and the human race, then that God's instructions for thriving as human beings should be

---

[334] Breggin, *Toxic Psychiatry*, 95-96.

[335] Idan Sharon, Roni Sharon, Svetlana Shteynman, "Shared Psychotic Disorder," ed. David Bienenfeld, *Medscape Online*, December 5, 2016, https://emedicine.medscape.com/ article/293107-overview.

considered authoritative. Acceptance of this premise (and any other explanation for that matter) does of course require faith just as the rejection of the premise requires faith.

In examining the Bible's assertions about the nature of truth, we learn that genuine truth is not produced in the human heart; it comes from God. Furthermore, the Bible teaches that this moral truth is the prescription for restoring the human soul. This perspective about the restorative nature of truth is evident in a prayer Jesus prayed for his followers in John 17:14-20:

> *Sanctify* [restore their souls] *them in the truth; your word is truth.* As you sent me into the world, so I have sent them into the world. And for their sake I consecrate myself, that they also may be sanctified in truth. I do not ask for these only, but also for those who will believe in me through their word [emphasis added]."

Here Christ relates several characteristics of truth that directly apply to the discussion on madness: (1) Faith is required to accept or reject spiritual truth that is not seen ("those who will believe in me through their word"). There are many truths about human nature and life that can be accepted only by faith, and right moral faith comes from hearing and hearing from the word of God (Romans 10:17).

The Bible also asserts that its truth is able to remedy humanity's deception. Psalm 19:7-8 provides one illustration; the original language literally says, "The Word of God is completely able to restore the soul to its original design; the truth the Bible reveals is consistently able and reliable to make those who are deceived into wise people." God's truth is spiritually healing and restorative to the soul. "Sanctify them in truth," is another way to say, restore or heal their soul with truth. When it comes to the problems of the soul—especially false fixed belief, the Bible insists that the Creator's wisdom is the standard of truth whereby deception must both be measured and remedied. John 8:31 declares it as such: "If you abide in my word, you are truly my disciples, and you will know the truth, and the truth will set you free."

(2) The Word of God is objective truth regarding human nature and the restoration of the soul/psyche. The Bible not only establishes a clear and unchangeable description of the incorporeal and moral aspect of human nature—a point that will be discussed further in the next chapter, it also insists that apart from God's insight, humanity cannot accurately discern or understand what is in the psyche. Jeremiah 17:9-10 explains,

> The heart is deceitful above all things, and desperately sick; who can understand it? "I the Lord search the heart and test the mind, to give every man according to his ways according to the fruit of his deeds.

If the very nature of man is deceitful, then how can he overcome his deceit—let alone spiritually peer into his immaterial soul—without relying on external and fixed truth? In contrast to Scripture, the secular theory of mental illness presupposes that people are by nature truthful.

Scripture also establishes that truth is not inwardly fixed or normative and that it must be pursued and obtained. King David asks God in Psalm 86:11a to "teach me your way, O Lord, that I may walk in your truth." Similarly, in Proverbs 23:23, the wise father admonishes his son to "buy truth, and do not sell it; buy wisdom, instruction, and understanding." We do not inherently possess truth—especially truth which requires faith to accept or reject, and so everyone must seek for truth. If truth is not objective, then again, no false fixed beliefs can exist and the theory of mental illness becomes a logical fallacy.

The Bible also states that entire multitudes can go mad or be perceived as mad. In Deuteronomy 28, the passage where God warned that He would strike the people with madness if His commandments were not accepted and obeyed is addressed to the entire nation of Israel. First Corinthians 14:23 is another example:

> If, therefore, the whole church comes together and all speak in tongues, and outsiders or unbelievers enter, will they not say that "you are *out of your minds* [lit. manic]?"

In this case, it is the minority—based upon their faith—judging the majority to be mad based upon observable yet unexplainable behavior. Isaiah 59:14-15a also notes how entire communities can forsake truth: "Justice is turned back, and righteousness stands far away; for truth has stumbled in the public squares, and uprightness cannot enter. Truth is lacking." A community, the majority, and utilitarianism are not reliable sources in determining truth or falsehood, and subsequently these objects of faith are not reliable in defining and explaining human nature.

CONCLUSION

What is believed to be true—both individually and corporately—about human nature will inevitably determine what mindsets and behaviors are considered as madness. Truth about human nature, what constitutes healthy faith, and what determines a sound mind, then, must objectively be established if madness is to be defined.

Because utilitarianism does not create or reveal truth, the majority can easily be deceived. In fact, deception often spreads through entire communities easier than truth does. Human nature, whether pertaining to the individual or to the community, is not naturally in truth and is, therefore, unreliable.

If truth is not objective, then madness cannot be either. If truth and falsehood are not objective, then objectively diagnosing others as insane is itself irrational and insanity.

In contrast to psychiatrists' ever-changing ideas of what constitutes truth, the Bible presents its perspective about reality that knocks against the modern perspective. In light of the current whirlwind of misinformation about the mind, the Bible's claims regarding immutable truth about human nature and what constitutes healthy, reliable, restorative faith should be considered, surprising though they may seem to some.

When truth is accepted to be objective, madness can then be defined with objectivity as observed throughout history. Yet if truth and madness are abstract and ever-changing concepts, then falsehood is too, and such a belief determines mental illness to only be an ever-changing subjective opinion—not something to be dogmatically imposed upon individuals and society. The undeniable fact that so many people are deceived and hurting, that they are truly delusional, however, is proof enough to accept that truth and falsehood are absolutes which must be understood and objectively defined if madness is to genuinely be remedied. Nonetheless, the one or the group of people who control concepts of truth regarding human nature and normalcy will inevitably control society's perspective of madness.

CHAPTER 6

STIGMATIZING MADNESS

"In a mode of thinking that emphasizes the unity of human nature, madness is not so much otherness as sameness."[336]
Petteri Pietikäinen, psychiatrist and historian

"We're all mad here. I'm mad. You're mad."
"How do you know I'm mad?" said Alice.
"You must be, "said the Cat, "or you wouldn't [be] here."[337]
Lewis Carroll, from *Alice's Adventures in Wonderland*

By their nature, truth and falsehood are antithetical, yet they must always be considered together since truth delineates falsehood. As noted in the previous chapter, an established standard of objective truth must precede any assertion of deviance or a suggestion of falsehood. In regard to mental illness, what one believes to be true about human nature (normalcy) ultimately determines how he/she defines mental illness. Professor of Psychology at Yale University Seymour Sarason states this reality well:

> Every psychologist has a picture of what man is or should be, of what society is or should be, and this picture infiltrates (indeed, is in part the

---

[336] Pietikäinen, *Madness,* 1.

[337] Lewis Carroll, *Alice's Adventures in Wonderland,* 1865 (Reprint, New York: Harvard University Press, 1998), 90.

> basis of) his or her theories, along with the psychologist's way of thinking about theory and practice.[338]

Professor of Psychiatry at the University of Texas Health Science Center Steven Pliszka also explains how psychiatric disorders are based upon ideas of normalcy: "In mental health, we define disorders as behavioral and psychological syndromes that deviate from some standard of normality (Angold et al., 1999, p. 58)."[339] Psychiatrist and author of *Listening to Prozac,* Peter Kramer, also observes, "How we see a person is a function of the categories we recognize—of our own private diagnostic system."[340] In other words, a person's beliefs about human nature ultimately determine how he/she judges another's faith—to be healthy or unhealthy, true or false. Those who are judged to be mentally ill are those who "have caused social disorganization by deviating too much from the accepted rules, they have been stigmatized—their identity is 'spoiled.'"[341] But without "accepted rules" being objectively established, there can be no deviance.

All theories and changes to definitions of madness which extend beyond the objective and historical definition, then, reflect differences in people's anthropology. This reality further explains why the construct of mental illness has become a broad and imprecise concept over the last century and why some historians suggest that the definition of madness varies across cultures and times:

> Just how bizarre or disruptive must someone's emotions or thought processes be before the label [of madness] is invoked? Self-evidently, that varies across time and place, across lines of gender, class, and so

---

338 Seymour B. Sarason, *Psychology Misdirected* (New York: Free Press, 1981), 154.

339 Steven R. Pliszka, *Treating ADHD and Comorbid Disorders: Psychosocial and Psychopharmacological Interventions* (New York: Guilford, 2009), 2.

340 Peter D. Kraemer, *Listening to Prozac* (New York: Penguin Books, 1997), 68.

341 Pietikäinen, *Madness,* 8.

> forth, albeit in non-random and sociologically explicable ways. . . . Are they part of a continuum of human psychopathology, or is there a sharp division observable here? Between madness and malingering, let us say, or between insanity and eccentricity, or between psychosis and neurosis? Historically, the verdict is varied.[342]

But as neurologist V.S. Ramachandran recognizes, odd or rare behavior does not truly define madness:

> There is a common tendency to equate "unusual" or "rare" with abnormal, but this is a logical fallacy. Genius is a rare but highly valued trait, whereas tooth decay is common but obviously undesirable.[343]

Rather than actually defining madness, what someone considers to be abnormal or bizarre is a reflection of that person's view of normalcy.

The evolutionary/humanistic theory of human nature carries the concept of madness beyond the objective definition and encourages evolutionists and materialists to utilize madness as a social construct to explain otherwise unexplainable human mindsets and behaviors. Such utility is the result of an anthropology which does not fully explain humanity;[344] it is not an accurate view of human nature.

Dr. Lawrie Reznek admits, however, that distinguishing normalcy from insanity is neither a scientific endeavor nor is it a simple task especially for theorists who do not hold to absolutes:

---

[342] Scull, *Madness*, 4.

[343] Ramachandran and Blakeslee, *Phantoms in the Brain*, 184-85.

[344] "Darwin's seminal publications in the nineteenth century laid the foundation for an evolutionary approach to psychology and psychiatry. Advances in 20th century evolutionary theory facilitated the development of evolutionary psychology and psychiatry as recognized areas of scientific investigation. In this century, advances in understanding the molecular basis of evolution, of the mind, and of psychopathology, offer the possibility of an integrated approach to understanding the proximal (psychobiological) and distal (evolutionary) mechanisms of interest to psychiatry and psychopharmacology" (D.J. Stein, "Evolutionary Theory, Psychiatry, and Psychopharmacology," *Progress in Neuro-Psychopharmacology and Biological Psychiatry* 5 [July 30, 2006]: 766-73, https://doi.org/10.1016/j.pnpbp.2006.01.003).

> Given that madness is the most severe of mental illnesses, and is recognized by the presence of delusions, we would hope delusions are easy to recognize. If they are not, then it will be difficult to decide who is mad and who is not. And if it is difficult to decide who has the most severe and obvious of all mental disorders—madness—what hope can there be to identify more subtle mental illnesses? For psychiatry's sake, one can only hope that identifying delusions is not a difficult matter. This hope is not well founded.[345]

It is not simply delusions or madness that have escaped psychiatrists' ability to objectively identify or define; normalcy itself, which should be the starting point, is still a mystery to leading theorists. Dr. Allen Frances states,

> "Mental disorder" and "normality" are both extremely protean concepts—each so amorphous, heterogeneous, and changeable in shape that we can never establish fixed boundaries between them. . . . Not having a useful definition of mental disorder creates a gaping hole at the center of psychiatric classifications.[346]

If secularists are unwilling or unable to objectively define and recognize delusions (false fixed beliefs that constitute madness) and unwilling or unable to define normalcy, then it is logical to conclude that they do not have a clear or accurate understanding of human nature. Yet this ambiguity or ignorance is precisely the position of modern theorists and many clinicians, and it is on this ambiguity that psychiatrists assert their place of authority over beliefs about human nature.[347] Frances comments on this common psychiatric perspective,

> The normal curve tells us a great deal about the distribution of everything from quarks to koalas, but it doesn't dictate to us where normal ends and abnormal begins. A ranting psychotic is far enough away from mean to be recognized as mentally sick by your aunt Tilly, but how do you decide when everyday anxiety or sadness is severe enough to be considered mental disorder? One thing does seem perfectly clear. On the statistical face of it, it is ridiculous to stretch

---

345 Reznek, *Delusions and Madness of the Masses*, preface xxvii.

346 Frances, *Saving Normal*, 16-17.

347 Lieberman, *Shrinks*, 87-88; 291.

> disorder so elastically that the near average person can qualify. Shouldn't most people be normal?[348]

Frances's last assertion explains an important presupposition that dominates modern secular theories of insanity: most of today's psychiatrists, neurologists, psychologists, and sociologists view madness/psychosis as a disorder or an abnormality. But what if madness is not an abnormality, and instead, "holding to false fixed beliefs despite clear evidence" describes normal human nature? Stated differently, what if all people are by nature disordered?

One of the most pressing anthropological questions that must be answered in regard to modern theories of madness is whether or not persistent false fixed beliefs, false sensory perceptions, and fragility are normal or abnormal to human nature. If false fixed beliefs or post-traumatic stress, as examples, are understood to be normal, a person must then conclude that all people are mad to some degree or assert a new understanding of madness beyond the historical definition. If all people are delusional, then the historical concept of madness explains normalcy and dismisses the notion that madness represents abnormal people. If people are by nature delusional, then labeling and categorizing only some delusions as mental illness stigmatizes people and, in turn, encourages the delusion that some deceived people are okay while others are not. Roy Porter contends,

> Setting the sick apart sustains the fantasy that we are whole. Disease diagnosis thus constitutes a powerful classificatory tool, and medicine contributes its fair share to the stigmatizing enterprise. Amongst those scapegoated and anathematized by means of this cognitive apartheid, the 'insane' have, of course, been conspicuous. The polarizing of the sane and the crazy in turn spurred and legitimized the institutionalizing trend.[349]

---

[348] Frances, *Saving Normal*, 8.

[349] Porter, *Madness*, 63.

Declaring only some delusions as abnormalities stigmatizes those who are most deceived, created the mental ward that sets the "insane" apart, and continues to sustain psychiatry's existence.

THE NORMALCY OF MADNESS

False fixed belief that is held despite clear available evidence not only defines madness; it also defines normalcy. People (individually and corporately) regularly divide over what they dogmatically believe to be true and what they sincerely perceive to be false. Some people rigidly believe that aliens or an explosion created planet Earth, while others place their faith in the biblical account of creation. Some pertinaciously argue that the world is billions of years old, while others understand it to be rather young—often times both parties use the same scientific evidence to defend their views (e.g., the Grand Canyon, sediment layers, and the fossil records). Many people around the world adamantly believe that Jesus Christ was merely a great rabbi who belongs in a group of unique deceased religious leaders throughout history, while millions of others unwaveringly believe that he rose from the dead and is the Savior of the world. Countless people are convinced that government agencies the world over are controlled by a secret society and unseen authority, while others view such a notion as a conspiracy theory and nothing more. Numerous people still believe that the world is flat, but such a view is in disagreement with the majority who hold the position that the earth is round. Some believe that life begins at birth, while others insist that a baby's life begins at conception. Still, other people attribute life's circumstances to luck, in contrast to others who believe that life's events unfold according to God's providence. In each of these cases (a few of countless examples available) one group believes a reality—often based upon indisputable evidence—while the other is delusional. Holding to false fixed beliefs despite clear available evidence, then, is not an abnormality but is a part of common human nature and a constant in every society.

Delusions are not merely commonplace in people throughout every society worldwide; they are also prevalent regarding theories of mental illness. Despite clear discrediting empirical evidence to the contrary, many people choose to hold to false fixed beliefs such as the theory of chemical imbalances being causative for constructs of mental illness. But this notion has been repudiated and rejected by prominent psychiatric theorists and researchers alike.[350] Take for example the testimony of Editor in Chief Emeritus of the *Psychiatric Times*, Ronald Pies:

> I am not one who easily loses his temper, but I confess to experiencing markedly increased limbic activity whenever I hear someone proclaim, "Psychiatrists think all mental disorders are due to a chemical imbalance!" In the past 30 years, I don't believe I have ever heard a knowledgeable, well-trained psychiatrist make such a preposterous claim, except perhaps to mock it. On the other hand, the "chemical imbalance" trope has been tossed around a great deal by opponents of psychiatry, who mendaciously attribute the phrase to psychiatrists themselves. And yes—the "chemical imbalance" image has been vigorously promoted by some pharmaceutical companies, often to the detriment of our patients' understanding. In truth, the "chemical imbalance" notion was always a kind of urban legend—never a theory seriously propounded by well-informed psychiatrists.[351]

Pharmacologist and researcher of internal medicine Peter Gotzche comments,

> One sign that psychiatry is in deep crisis is that more than half the patients believe their mental disorder is caused by a chemical imbalance in the brain. They have this misperception from their doctors, which means that more than half the psychiatrists lie to their patients. I know of no other specialty whose practitioners lie to their patients. Psychiatrists also lie to themselves and to the public.[352]

---

[350] For further study on the disproven chemical imbalance theory, see Berger, *Influence of Nurture*, 63-68 and Berger, *Necessity for Dependence*, 28-33.

[351] Ronald Pies, "Psychiatry's New Brain-Mind and the Legend of the 'Chemical Imbalance,'" *Psychiatric Times*, July 11, 2011, http://www.psychiatric times.com/blogs/psychiatry-new-brain-mind-and-legend-chemical-imbalance.

[352] Gotzsche, *Deadly Psychiatric and Organised Denial*, Loc 164.

Despite dozens of prominent psychiatrists' testimonies and the overwhelming empirical evidence now available to show the absurdity of the chemical imbalance trope, some who are faced with irrefutable evidence cannot let go of their false fixed beliefs and still insist that the chemical imbalance theory is true. It is equally perplexing that many psychiatrists continue to utilize a known delusion in attempt to treat delusions/madness.

False fixed beliefs are an intricate part of human nature and not an abnormality. Labeling someone as mad or mentally ill, then, does not identify an abnormal person or someone with an abnormality as today's psychiatric theory suggests; it simply exposes a negative characteristic of human nature (deception) which is difficult to explain or resolve within a humanistic worldview. This human attribute though, is unpleasant, impairing, destructive, and often manifests itself in morally and culturally unacceptable ways.

When deception becomes egregious, impairing, threatening, or impossible to ignore, it is framed as something outside of human nature. This common practice has come to be how many people incorrectly define madness. People would rather believe that others are mad and not themselves, and defining or restricting madness to represent delusions that seemingly cannot be explained, are horrific, or are clearly destructive serves to ease the burden of many in society to acknowledge and deal with their own deeply deceived and impaired nature.

Since at its core madness historically has been defined by false fixed beliefs, normal and abnormal beliefs must be determined and clearly proved. Dr. Pietikäinen explains,

> Madness can be understood only in terms of degree, and of the prevailing medical and cultural beliefs about human nature, normality, and deviance.[353]

But are there clear differences between false fixed beliefs which are framed as abnormal and delusions which are said to be

---

[353] Pietikäinen, *Madness*, 3.

normal? Do abnormal false beliefs even exist? Are people naturally born into truth or falsehood? A still more pressing question is who has the right and is best equipped to both recognize and determine which beliefs society should view as false and what beliefs should be accepted as true about human nature?

A Common Historical Perspective

Many people throughout history have recognized that madness (deep impairing deceit) is a foundational aspect of all humanity and not a category to stigmatize a few. The Dutch humanist philosopher Desiderius Erasmus said in 1509,

> I doubt if a single individual could be found from the whole of mankind free from some form of insanity. The only difference is one of degree. A man who sees a gourd and takes it for his wife is called insane because this happens to very few people.[354]

Johann Wolfgang von Goethe also stated, "We do not have to visit a madhouse to find disordered minds; our planet is the mental institution of the universe."[355] Similarly, Mark Twain once suggested,

> Let us consider that we are all partially insane. It will explain us to each other; it will unriddle many riddles; it will make clear and simple many things which are involved in haunting and harassing difficulties and obscurities now.[356]

Renowned psychiatrists, such as Karl Menninger (1950), agree:

> Gone forever is the notion that the mentally ill person is an exception. It is now accepted that most people have some degree of mental illness

---

[354] Desiderius Erasmus, *Praise of Folly* (1509), chapter 38. See also Rosemarie Jarski, *Words from the Wise: Over 6,000 of the Smartest Things Ever Said* (New York: Skyhorse Publishing, 2007), 312.

[355] Johann Wolfgang von Goethe quoted by Reznek, *Delusions and Madness of the Masses*, 47.

[356] Mark Twain, *Christian Science* (New York: Harper, 1907), chapter 5.

at some time, and many of them have a degree of mental illness most of the time.[357]

Psychiatrist and historian of madness Petteri Pietikäinen concurs,

> Some of us are completely crazy, others completely sane, but most of us occupy the grey zone where we are mad at some times, neurotic at other times and, most of the time, not so sure whether our minds are truly in order or not.[358]

If insanity is defined objectively and historically, then the modern construct of mental illness ceases to be a valid identifier of abnormalities or disorder. Instead, mental illness describes an ugly and destructive truth about what it means to be human. As psychiatrist Harry Stack Sullivan once said about his own anthropology that governed his psychiatric practice, "We shall assume that everyone is much more simply human than otherwise."[359] Madness, no matter how deep and impairing, is a normal aspect of human nature.

A Debated Psychiatric Perspective

The psychiatric and humanistic perspective on what constitutes normalcy is not well-defined, and thus a great deal of disagreement exists. Some professionals believe that constructs of mental illness represent human abnormalities or biological diseases, while others understand that the current suggested psychiatric disorders simply represent constructs which explain various negative, impairing, and persistent aspects of human nature.

---

[357] Menninger, *Vital Balance*, 33.

[358] Pietikäinen, *Madness*, 4.

[359] Harry Stack Sullivan, *Interpersonal Theory of Psychiatry* (New York: W.W. Norton Company, 1953), 32.

The Abnormal View

It can be said with great reliability that most psychiatrists and clinicians believe that the concept of mental illness identifies people who are abnormal or disordered. Accordingly, psychiatrists and other theorists have utilized the construct of mental illness to represent a category which explains mindsets and behaviors that fall outside of an evolutionary anthropology but still must be explained. In this view, madness represents an almost non-human category to explain seemingly otherwise unexplainable aspects of human nature.

More specifically, evolutionists do not accept human morality/depravity and human fragility as explanatory for impairing and destructive mindsets and behaviors; they believe that people are neither morally responsible (sinful) or normally weak for lengths of time. It is on this premise that those who are struggling with specific—albeit common—delusions and hallucinations, who are naturally depraved, or who have ongoing distress are categorized, stigmatized, and judged within humanistic thinking and psychiatric theory to be abnormal. After asserting that no precise definition of mental illness exists, the APA states in the *DSM-5* that

> a mental disorder is a syndrome characterized by clinically significant disturbance in an individual's cognition, emotion regulation, or behavior that reflects a dysfunction in the psychological, biological, or developmental processes underlying mental functioning. [360]

The common psychiatric belief is that mental processes and behaviors which are impairing, distressful, or morally reprehensible should be considered disturbances or dysfunctions. In fact, as respected psychiatrist Bessel van der Kolk recognizes, today's prominent secular theorists consider immoral mindsets and behaviors to be disorders:

> Now a new paradigm was emerging: Anger, lust, pride, greed, avarice, and sloth—as well as all the other problems we humans have always

[360] APA, *DSM-5*, 20.

struggled to manage—were recast as "disorders" that could be fixed by the administration of appropriate chemicals.[361]

If people are all sinners as the Bible claims (Romans 3:23), then all people are disordered. Dr. Allen Frances candidly remarks,

> Binge eating was once considered a sin; should it now be a psychiatric disorder? Is the forgetting of old age an illness or just old age? Is having sex with a teenager just a crime or also a sign of craziness? And in evaluating any given person, we lack a general definition of mental disorder to help us decide whether he is normal or a patient, mad or bad.[362]

These common confessions have led many people to acknowledge that psychiatry is really a moral endeavor:

> Psychiatry's crisis is not simply a problem of diagnostic precision or of misplaced economic priorities; it is also a moral predicament that reflects our times.[363]

Without establishing an objective and clear standard of normalcy, psychiatrists can continue to frame undesirable or seemingly unexplainable and destructive mindsets and behaviors as abnormalities. In doing so, they informally reveal their view of what it means to be normal, and unfortunately, they create a false and impairing identity in those whom they set aside and categorize as abnormal. Dr. Porter explains, "Stigmatizing—the creation of spoiled identity—involves projecting onto an individual or group judgments as to what is inferior, repugnant, or disgraceful."[364] The stigmatizing nature of categorizing people as abnormal creates a self-fulfilling prophecy and further promotes delusional thinking. It is obvious to those acquainted with someone who has received and accepted a psychiatric label that stigmatization spoils the identity.

---

361 Van der Kolk, *Body Keeps the Score*, 27.

362 Frances, *Saving Normal*, 17.

363 Pettus, "Psychiatry by Prescription."

364 Porter, *Madness*, 62.

The APA must avoid objectively defining both sanity and mental illness, as doing so would expose today's Kraepelinian theory and system of mental health to largely be a delusion. Still, the APA insists that the *DSM-5* provides the best resource to determine the difference between normalcy and madness. They do recognize, however, that the *DSM-5* is imprecise and controversial and that alleged abnormalities cannot be objectively determined.[365] This reality has led many like historian Andrew Scull to suggest that the APA's anthropology is an ever-changing fantasy:

> Despite the frantic and endlessly repeated efforts of the committees charged with writing and re-writing the Bible of psychiatric practice, the *DSM* of the American Psychiatric Association, the boundary between sanity and madness remains permeable and contested, and the pretensions to have cut nature at the joints in differentiating hundreds of types and subtypes of mental disorder are exactly that, *an elaborately disguised game of make-believe* [emphasis added].[366]

If false faith and false perceptions are part of normal human nature, then the concept of mental illness as an abnormality or as a unique disease is shown to be itself a false fixed belief. Such a revelation would not only undermine current theories of mental illness, but it would also dismiss as false the evolutionary anthropology which teaches that humanity is naturally strong (able to endure and mentally handle ongoing distress and impairment) and without natural deep-seated falsehood.

When truth about human nature and character cannot be explained or remedied within one's worldview, labeling people as abnormal or as "monsters"[367] and setting them aside becomes

---

[365] "In the absence of clear biological markers or clinically useful measurements of severity for many mental disorders, it has not been possible to completely separate normal and pathological [abnormal] symptom expressions contained in the diagnostic criteria" (APA, *DSM-5*, 21).

[366] Scull, *Madness*, 4-5.

[367] Robert Berezin, "Reflections on the 'Moral Monsters' Dominating the News): (https://www.medscape.com/viewarticle/891927?nlid=120668_424&src=WNL_mdplsfeat_180213_mscpedit_psyc&uac=264124BV&spon=12&impID=1558455&faf=1#vp_2).

necessary to sustain false beliefs. As a result, psychiatry has transformed madness into a social construct that stigmatizes people rather than helping them to return to truth. This cycle of labeling, separating, and medicating the allegedly abnormal creates a damaging self-fulfilling prophecy that is wreaking havoc on both individuals and society.

The Normal View

Many prominent and respected secular professionals throughout history, however, have recognized that deep impairing deception characterizes normal human nature. In their view, madness is not something outside of normalcy; the term rather exposes an ugly aspect of humanity that is difficult to accept. Scull explains, "Perhaps madness has meaning and reveals something central about ourselves and our very identity as human beings."[368] Scull writes elsewhere,

> Paradoxically, madness exists not just in opposition to civilization, or solely on its margins. On the contrary, it has been a central topic of concern for artists, for dramatists, novelists, composers, divines, and physicians and scientists, not to mention how closely it affects almost all of us—either through our own encounters with disturbances of reason and emotion, or through those of family members and friends. *In important ways, that is, madness is indelibly part of civilization, not located outside it.* It is a problem that insistently invades our consciousness and our daily lives. It is thus at once luminal and anything but. Madness is a disturbing subject, one whose mysteries puzzle us still. *The loss of reason, the sense of alienation from the common-sense world the rest of us imagine we inhabit,* the shattering emotional turmoil that seizes hold of some of us and will not let go: *these are a part of our shared human experience down through the centuries and in every culture. Insanity haunts the human imagination. . . . It reminds insistently of how tenuous our own hold on reality may sometimes be. It challenges our sense of the very limits of what it is to be human.* [emphases added][369]

Others, such as clinical psychologist Richard Bentall, suggest that "psychosis shines a particularly penetrating light on ordinary human functioning. Indeed, I do not think it is an exaggeration to say that the study of psychosis amounts to the

---

[368] Scull, *Madness*, 5.

[369] Ibid., 10.

study of human nature."[370] Former head of psychiatry at Duke University Medical School and chair of the *DSM-IV* task force, Allen Frances, comments on some of the new constructs in the *DSM-5*:

> *DSM-5* has included several sure-fire fads of the future. All have symptoms that are part of everyday life and commonly encountered in the general population. None has a definition precise enough to prevent the mislabeling of many people now considered normal. None has a treatment proven to be effective. All will likely lead to much unnecessary, and sometimes harmful, treatment or testing. The aggregate effects will be overdiagnosis, unnecessary stigma, overtreatment, a misallocation of resources, and *a negative impact in the way we see ourselves as individuals and as a society* [emphasis added].[371]

The historian Roy Porter remarks in a similar fashion,

> More people than ever swallow the medications, and perhaps even the theories, which psychiatry prescribes, and attend various sorts of therapists, *as the idioms of the psychological and the psychiatric replace Christianity and humanism as the ways of making sense of self*—to oneself, one's peers, and the authorities [emphasis added].[372]

"The way we see ourselves" or "the ways of making sense of self" are both ways of expressing one's anthropology/one's view of normalcy. Historian and psychiatrist Petteri Pietikäinen concurs:

> When we study madness we simultaneously study human nature. Definitions of and criteria for madness change temporarily and locally. Through studying violations of the boundaries of normality and sanity we can illuminate the mysteries of the human condition. The starting point of my book is the assumption that culture shapes madness, but I also subscribe to the view that madness shapes culture by impacting the ways in which we understand ourselves, our fellow humans and the surrounding reality. For this reason, to study madness historically is to study intellectual and the socio-cultural changes that constitute varieties of human experience.[373]

---

370 Bentall, *Madness Explained,* 111.

371 Frances, *Saving Normal*, 176.

372 Roy Porter, *Madness*, 217-18.

373 Pietikäinen, *Madness*, 7.

Psychiatrist Robert Berezin also agrees,

> Psychiatry has lost its way and has become a distribution center for psychiatric drugs. It needs to face that psychiatric problems and symptoms are human problems, no more and no less, derived from the formation of our characters as we adapt to our emotional environments.[374]

Still other professors of psychiatry conclude that psychosis is simply a picture of normal dilemmas experienced by so-called ordinary people.[375] Madness is not a category outside of normalcy but an intricate, yet destructive, aspect of what it means to be human. Those who attempt to use madness as an identifier of human abnormality, in truth, expose their own inability to fully and properly explain human nature from their accepted worldview.

THE NORMALCY OF CORE ELEMENTS

In order to realize more fully whether madness is normal or a construct which explains abnormal people, the foundational elements must be examined more carefully to determine whether or not these characteristics define human nature or expose disorders. If faith, deception, and ongoing mental fragility are common, then madness should not be utilized as a social construct to describe alleged human abnormalities or diseases. Instead, madness continues to be, as the historical record attests, a description of impairing and destructive deceit that has gripped the hearts of all people.

---

374 Robert Berezin, "Reflections on the 'Moral Monsters' Dominating the News," *Medscape Psychiatry Online* (February 1, 2018): (https://www.medscape.com/viewarticle/891927?nlid=120668_424&src=WNL_mdplsfeat_180213_mscpedit_psyc&uac=264124BV&spon=12&impID=1558455&faf=1#vp_2).

375 Michael Musalek, P. Berner, and H. Katschnig, "Delusional Theme, Sex and Age," *Psychopathology* 22 (1989): 260-67.

Falsehood

Human nature does not naturally accept truth; instead, people tend to dogmatically embrace falsehood. Prominent evolutionary biologist Robert Trivers asserts that by the time children are six months old they have begun to use deception in order to get their way or fulfill their own desires,

> After birth, the first clear signs of deception come about age 6 months, which is when the child fakes need when there appears to be no good reason. The child will scream and bawl, roll on the floor in apparent agony and yet stop within seconds after the audience leaves the room, only to resume within seconds when the audience is back. Later, the child will hide objects from the view of others and deny that it cares about a punishment when it clearly does. So-called 'white lies', of the sort "The meal you served was delicious" appear after age 5.[376]

Psychiatrist Laurie Reznek comments on how controlled studies repeatedly provide empirical evidence which show how all people are naturally delusional:

> Evidence abounds to show that normal people cling to cherished but false beliefs and are extremely resistant to giving them up even when there is a better theory available. This evidence comes from at least three different sources—anecdotal accounts of individuals clinging irrationally to false beliefs, experimental studies that show that people cling to beliefs even when they have obvious evidence to the contrary, and case studies of groups of people clinging to empirically unsupported beliefs. Starting with anecdotal evidence, all of us have encountered normal people who, in the grip of powerful emotions, seem to hang on to erroneous beliefs in the face of obvious evidence to the contrary. For example, a mother clings to her belief that her son is innocent (in spite of the fact that the police have his fingerprints on the murder weapon) because it is too emotionally difficult for her to contemplate the possibility that she has brought a murderer into the world. We might say quite correctly that she is deluding herself. Such episodes of self-delusion are commonplace. We all find it difficult to accept certain truths, and delude ourselves into believing in a glaring falsehood in spite of evidence to the contrary.[377]

---

[376] Gareth Cook, "The Hidden Logic of Deception," *Scientific America Online*, December 27, 2011, https://www.scientificamerican.com/article /hdiden-logic-deception/.

[377] Reznek, *Delusions and Madness of the Masses*, 48-49.

In her book *A Mind of Its Own: How Your Brain Distorts and Deceives You*, psychologist and neuroscientist Cordelia Fine describes how pride/vanity is normative and part of self-deception:

> When life or psychology researchers are kind enough to leave the reasons for success or failure ambiguous, the self-serving bias is readily and easily engaged to protect and nurture the ego. However, our vain [minds] aren't completely impervious to reality. . . . *When we lose all sight of our ugly face in reality's mirror, it generally means that we have also lost hold of our sanity* [emphasis added]. On the other hand, who wants to see the warts and all with pristine clarity? . . . By calling on powerful biases in memory and reasoning, the brain can selectively edit and censor the truth, both about ourselves and the world, making for a softer, kinder, and altogether more palatable reality.[378]

Psychiatrist Satel and psychologist Lilienfeld are also convinced of humanity's deceptive nature and claim that the brain should be understood as the "organ of deceit."[379]

Psychiatrists and psychologists are not alone in recognizing that people are normally deceived. Neurologists and neuroscientists have made deception a priority in their research. Neurologist David Eagleman, for one, comments on the deceptive nature of memories:

> Our past is not a faithful record. Instead it's a reconstruction, and sometimes it can border on mythology. When we review our life memories, we should do so with the awareness that not all the details are accurate. Some came from stories that people told us about ourselves; others were filled in with what we thought must have happened. So if your answer to who you are is based simply on your memories, that makes your identity something of a strange, ongoing, mutable narrative.[380]

Eagleman later writes, "Not only is it possible to implant false new memories in the brain [the mind], but people embraced and

---

[378] Cordelia Fine, *A Mind of Its Own: How Your Brain Distorts and Deceives* (New York: W. W. Norton and Company, 2006), 8.

[379] Sally Satel and Scott Lilienfeld, *Brainwashed: The Seductive Appeal of Mindless Neuroscience* (New York: Basic Books, 2013), 80.

[380] David Eagleman, *The Brain: The Story of You* (New York: Pantheon Books, 2015), 26.

embellished them, unknowingly weaving fantasy into the fabric of their identity."[381] Other controlled studies reveal how people can even create entire events in their imagination which never occurred.[382] Similarly, *Scientific American* published an interview in which the authors state,

> We lie to ourselves all the time. We tell ourselves that we are better than average—that we are more moral, more capable, less likely to become sick or suffer an accident. It's an odd phenomenon, and an especially puzzling one to those who think about our evolutionary origins. Self-deception is so pervasive that it must confer some advantage. But how could we be well served by a brain [mind] that deceives us?[383]

Nobel Prize winner, neuroscientist, and molecular biologist Francis Crick also comments on humanity's true nature,

> [Humans have] *an almost limitless capacity for self-deception* [emphasis added]. The very nature of our brains—evolved to guess the most plausible interpretations of the limited evidence available—makes it almost inevitable that, without the discipline of scientific research, we shall often jump to wrong conclusions, especially about rather abstract matters.[384]

Clearly, even accomplished scientists and physicians recognize that human nature is burdened with "an almost limitless capacity for self-deception." Being deceived—even being overtaken by deception—is not an abnormality.

Though Crick suggests that science is the remedy to self-deception and that the brain is responsible for false faith, much of what is called science within theories of mental illness has proved to be false. But again, psychiatry itself rests on the "faulty science" of phrenology (the belief that the skull

---

381 Ibid., 25.

382 "False Memories," *Psychologist World Online*, https://www.psychologistworld.com/memory/false-memories-questioning-eyewitness-testimony.

383 Cook, "Hidden Logic of Deception."

384 Crick, *Astonishing Hypothesis*, 262.

determined mental faculties, personality, behaviors, and character).[385]

The construct of science is further evidence that truth is not subjective/relative and is not naturally a part of human nature: All people must pursue and discover what is true; truth is not inherently possessed. In fact, one of the most prominent of all American scientific theorists Karl Popper once asserted that "science must begin with myths, and with the criticism of myths."[386] At the very core of the scientific method is the reality that deception and falsehood are obstacles that people must overcome. This fact exposes that every human pursuit of truth, including the pursuit of truth about the physical world, is hindered by our own innate falsehood. Faith is required to make sense of the natural world and even more important to discern the spiritual realm/incorporeal realties.

Faith/Beliefs/Perceptions

Despite faith's centrality to the concept of madness and to the human soul and outworking behavior, many secularists wish to minimize or deny the importance of faith in human nature—especially as it relates to madness. Atheist philosopher Friedrich Nietzche regularly attempted to dismiss faith as necessary or relevant to explain or remedy behavior, and ironically, he tried to use madness as evidence against the importance of religious faith: "A casual stroll through the lunatic asylum shows that faith does not prove anything."[387] Though he attempted to discredit the importance of religious faith and narrow his focus on observable behavior, Nietzche overlooked the true nature of

---

385 Group for the Advancement of Psychiatry, "The History of Psychiatry 19th Century," 3:44.

386 Karl Popper, *Philosophy of Science: An Historical Anthology*, ed. Timothy McGrew, Marc Alsperctor-Kelly, and Fritz Allhoff (New York: Wiley and Sons, 2009), 480.

387 Friedrich Nietzche, http://www.atheistrepublic.com/gallery/faith-does-not-prove-anything-nietzsche.

madness: the reason so many people end up in asylums or mental wards is their false fixed beliefs. Faith is not the problem; false faith is. In fact, former president of the American Psychology association John Norcross (along with many other clinicians) remarks on how scientific research proves that intrinsic faith promotes mental health:

> People who are intrinsically religious have a personalized religious commitment and view their faith as an end in itself, while people who are extrinsically religious view their faith as a means to other ends (for example, social affiliation). Intrinsic are more likely than the extrinsic and the "indiscriminately proreligious" to be mentally healthy (Batson, Schoenrade, and Ventis, 1991: Gartner, 1996).[388]

Faith is a foundational aspect of human nature, so it is no wonder that false faith is an essential feature of insanity. Dr. Reznek explains, "To understand delusions, then, we must have some understanding of the nature of beliefs. Beliefs are commonplace and we all have them."[389] These beliefs are normal non-physical aspects of our character that manifest in behavior; they define us, bring hope, sustain identity and relationships, and determine responses to circumstances and our moral behavior.

Beliefs are not only a foundational aspect of human nature, but they also reveal our soul's relationship to objective truth and thus our morality. This fact is why madness exists: people recognize that falsehood is destructive (it is bad) and must be remedied and that truth is vital to a good life and a healthy society. Furthermore, the constructs of delusions, psychosis, and schizophrenia highlight the reality that people's faith (not their biology) determines their moral behavior and ability/inability to endure hardships. Atheist and neuroscientist Sam Harris writes in his book, *The End of Faith*,

---

[388] John Norcross, Everett L. Worthington, Jr., and Steven J. Sandage, *Psychotherapy Relationships That Work: Therapist Contributions and Responsiveness to Patients* (New York: Oxford University Press, 2002), 384.

[389] Reznek, *Delusions and Madness of the Masses*, preface xviii.

> Your beliefs define your vision of the world; they dictate your behavior; they determine your emotional responses to other human beings. . . . They become part of the very apparatus of your mind, determining your desires, fears, expectations and subsequent behavior.[390]

Beliefs define not only our "vision of the world," but also our view of human nature. Dr. Reznek likewise relates how faith is essential to who we are as people:

> Beliefs, then, have two important properties. They aim at the truth, and they explain our behavior. These two important properties of beliefs are related. Beliefs purport to be true descriptions of reality and it is only because they have this property that they influence our behavior.[391]

A cursory study of the placebo and nocebo effects illustrate faith's ability not only to produce behavior, but also to alter the human body and provide physical healing.[392]

Though many psychiatrists insist that psychosis differs from "normal imaginations" based upon whether or not someone can or cannot help their own false thinking,[393] there exists no empirical means to discern this condition, and usually, the testimony of the person diagnosed as psychotic is the entire basis of determination. But there is a serious problem with accepting the testimony of people identified as being deceitful (delusional): their testimonies are not reliable. The studies conducted by David Rosenhan involving "pseudo-patients" who pretended to

---

390 Sam Harris, *The End of Faith: Religion, Terror, and the Future of Reason* (New York: Norton and Company, 2005), 12.

391 Reznek, *Delusions and Madness of the Masses*, preface xx.

392 Berger, *Reality of the Physical Nature*, 141-51.

393 "There is a world of difference between the voluntary, playful engagement of the imagination, and the involuntary descent into psychosis" Ronald Pies, "Confusing Psychosis with imagination," *Psychiatric Times Online* (November 3, 2017): http://www.psychiatrictimes.com/schizophrenia/confusing-psychosis-imagination/?rememberme=1&elq_mid=228&elq_cid=893295&GUID=31158D64-F01A-4DEA-AC1A-D3CE843FC9BC.

be schizophrenic and deceived doctors prove this point handily.[394]

In short, faith is an inescapable part of being human; it determines how we behave and how we relate to truth. If absolute truth does not exist, then neither does absolute falsehood. To accept the notion that truth about human nature and the psyche/soul is not immutable is to also embrace as illogical the concept of psychosis/madness.

Even reason—the human ability to rationalize—is determined by our beliefs. Reznek remarks,

> We frequently 'observe' ourselves to have reasons for our actions when these are best viewed as rationalizations. Reasons are those beliefs that actually affect our behavior, and rationalizations are those beliefs that we tell ourselves we hold because it is easier for us to accept that our behavior is motivated by noble reasons rather than base ones.[395]

It is logical to conclude, then, that false beliefs would produce irrational thoughts and yield unreasonable behavior. It is also reasonable to accept that false fixed beliefs are a common problem in the hearts of all humanity and that the moral nature of people determines their motives, affects their reasoning, and explains their moral behavior.

Those who believe in the biomedical model of madness attempt to differentiate between normal and abnormal false beliefs without empirical evidence or logical reason to do so:

> Unfortunately, clinicians and researchers schooled in the biomedical approach to psychiatry have often assumed that delusions and ordinary beliefs are completely different.[396]

Faith is so important to practical living that someone's worldview even determines how that person interprets and approaches another's false beliefs.

---

[394] See David Rosenhan's experiment on schizophrenia: "On Being Sane in Insane Places," *Science* 179, no. 4070 (January 19, 1973): 250-58.

[395] Reznek, *Delusions and Madness of the Masses*, preface xx.

[396] Bentall, *Madness Explained*, 302.

While psychiatrists insist that hallucinations are a separate criterion from delusions, hallucinations are simply false beliefs about physical stimuli—what the APA refers to as "false sensory perceptions." Whereas delusions are false beliefs about spiritual, abstract, or incorporeal matters (e.g., a person's belief that aliens are coming to take over the earth), hallucinations are false beliefs about physical stimuli (e.g., a person's belief that they see a dead body at the foot of the bed when none exists). Once again, the differing content or nature of false fixed beliefs is cause for psychiatrists to separate delusions and hallucinations into allegedly unique criteria. Without realizing it, psychiatrists' division of false beliefs by their content in this way attests to humanity's dual nature.

Like delusions, hallucinations are not abnormalities or signs of abnormalities. The book *Mental Illness: The Reality of the Physical Nature,*[397] in part, explains how hallucinations are normal human experiences that expose the deceived nature of all people. Prior to his death, neurologist and Professor of Psychiatry Norman Sacks also wrote a book, *Hallucinations,* in which he explained from a medical perspective how hallucinations are normal: "Hallucinatory experiences," he says, are "an essential part of the human condition."[398] He also notes that distinguishing between hallucinations, misperceptions, and illusions is not so easy—if a distinction exists at all:

> Hallucinations may overlap with misperceptions or illusions. If, looking at someone's face, I see only half a face, this is a misperception. The distinction becomes less clear with more complex situations.[399]

In truth, "misperception" is another way to describe false perception. Neurologist V.S. Ramachandran offers his own take on the visual hallucinations experienced during psychosis: "All these bizarre visual hallucinations are simply an exaggerated

---

397 Berger, *Reality of the Physical Nature*.

398 Sacks, *Hallucinations*, preface xiv.

399 Ibid., preface x.

version of the processes that occur in your brain [mind] and mine every time we let our imagination run free."[400] In many ways, our imagination attests to the human ability to think beyond reality and form our own narratives according to our own desires or fears. Similarly, neurologist David Eagleman comments on how people create their own sensory reality,

> Despite the simplicity of that assembly-line model of vision, it's incorrect. In fact, the brain [the mind] generates its own reality, even before it receives information coming in from the eyes and the other senses. This is known as the internal model.[401]

Dr. Ramachandran likewise remarks about visual perceptions:

> Every act of perception, even something as simple as viewing a drawing of a cube, involves an act of *judgment* by the brain. In making these *judgments*, the brain takes advantage of the fact that the world we live in is not chaotic and amorphous; it has stable physical properties. During evolution—and partly during childhood as a result of learning—these stable properties become incorporated into the visual areas of the brain as certain "assumptions" or *hidden knowledge* about the world that can be used to eliminate ambiguity in perception [emphasis added].[402]

Each of these psychiatrists and neurologists concur that hallucinations are indeed a normal part of human nature. The "'assumptions' or hidden knowledge about the world" is another way to describe one's worldview. Underlying faith will determine how a person not only views the world but also how that individual perceives the physical world.

---

[400] Ramachandran and Blakeslee, *Phantoms in the Brain*, 111.

[401] Eagleman, *Brain*, 51.

[402] Ramachandran and Blakeslee, *Phantoms in the Brain*, 67-68.

Lack of sleep, traumatic experiences,[403] valid physical diseases, psychoactive substances,[404] the death of a loved one,[405] and every day sensory processes (to name a few) do not produce falsehood, they simply better expose how deceived humanity is. In truth, all people are naturally deceived about both spiritual and physical realities, and some become so deceived that they deny many realities and create fantasies as an attempt to endure. In large part, an individual's worldview (underlying beliefs) determines whether he/she embraces truth or turns to falsehood.

Fragility

Although the historical definition of madness exposes human depravity to be a core element of insanity/mental illness, today's psychiatric theorists assert that human fragility should also be considered as an important component of mental illness. In their perspective on mankind, both depravity and fragility are abnormalities.

As previously noted, most mental health professionals do not believe that humanity struggles with fragility for long periods of time, and thus they categorize ongoing distress and impairment as mental disorders. *Mental Illness: The Necessity for Faith and Authority* discusses in detail how chair of the *DSM-III* task force Bob Spitzer altered the Kraepelinian construct of mental illness by introducing two subjective criteria, which clinicians now use in determining alleged abnormalities.[406] Those criteria are "significant distress" and the persistence or enduring

---

403 APA, *DSM-5*, 104.

404 Ibid., 110.

405 Ronald Pies and Cynthia Geppert, "'Clinical Depression' or 'Life Sorrows'? Distinguishing between Grief and Depression in Pastoral Care," *Ministry Magazine*, May 2015, 8. See also Sacks, *Hallucinations*, 212.

406 Berger, *Necessity for Faith and Authority*, 71-81.

nature of the distress or impairment.[407] The assumption Spitzer imposed and most psychiatrists continue to make is that any ongoing mental impairment, distress, or deception qualifies people as being mentally ill. For example, respected researcher for the NIMH and Professor of Healthcare Policy at Harvard University Ronald Kessler comments on how anxiety is a normal distressful mindset, which psychiatrists have transformed into an abnormality: "To say that 28 percent of Americans have anxiety disorders assumes that being anxious is like having cancer. But anxiety is part of being human."[408] Former Research Professor of Psychology at Harvard University Jerome Kagan also remarks,

> We could get philosophical and ask ourselves: "What does mental illness mean?" . . . Describing every child who is depressed or anxious as being mentally ill is ridiculous. Adolescents are anxious, that's normal. They don't know what college to go to. Their boyfriend or girlfriend just stood them up. Being sad or anxious is just as much a part of life as anger or sexual frustration.[409]

Though mental processes such as anxiety and depression are normal, viewing distress and impairment as abnormalities if they persist has become the common psychiatric perspective in today's society.

Many of today's constructs of mental illness contained in the *DSM-5* exist simply because they are common human behavior and ways of thinking that are viewed as ongoing impairment or distress. They reside in the *DSM-5*, not because they are abnormalities, but because the APA has denied that they are normal human responses to life's adversities. Such a position assumes an anthropology which suggests that normal people are not impaired or distressed for lengthy periods of time. This now common belief is the product of society's acceptance of the evolutionary theory; humanity is believed to be strong, and

---

407 APA, *DSM-5*, 20.

408 Ronald C. Kessler quoted by Pettus, "Psychiatry by Prescription."

409 Kagan, "Tutoring Instead of Pills?"

depravity and fragility are unacceptable ways of viewing normal human mindsets, behaviors, and emotions.

One clear illustration of this wrong anthropology and the utility of madness to sustain its acceptance is the psychiatric construct of "post-traumatic stress disorder" (PTSD). Psychiatrists have convinced much of society that those who endure severe trauma or are unable to mentally bear the burden of life's difficulties and stresses are mentally ill. Dr. Frances expounds upon this common psychiatric belief:

> The definitions of mental disorder generally require the presence of distress, disability, dysfunction, dyscontrol [sic], and/or disadvantage. This sounds better as alliteration than it works as operational guide. How much distress, disability, dysfunction, dyscontrol [sic], and disadvantage must there be, and of what kind?[410]

The premise which views post-traumatic stress as a disorder rests on the false belief that people are normally capable of enduring severe trauma or stress without lasting, deep, and impairing mental and behavioral struggles. Yet, as holocaust survivor and psychiatrist Viktor Frankl once wrote, "An abnormal reaction to an abnormal situation is normal behavior."[411] American author Philip Dick understands this normal human tendency: "It is sometimes an appropriate response to reality to go insane."[412] Instead of changing their beliefs to better reflect true human nature, secular theorists of madness choose instead to devise constructs in attempt to explain unpleasant or seemingly unsolvable human struggles into their false anthropological beliefs. They must do so, since their anthropology is unable to explain distressful, immoral, destructive, or debilitating mental processes otherwise.

In truth, the evolutionary theory has no room within its proposed anthropology to view mankind as immoral, fragile,

---

410 Frances, *Saving Normal*, 16.

411 Viktor E. Frankl, *Man's Search for Meaning* (Boston: Beacon Press, 2006), 38.

412 Philip K. Dick quoted by Eiss, *Insanity and Genius*, 599.

dependent upon faith, or so deceived that people are capable of the most bizarre and evil mindsets and behaviors imaginable. Yet, these realities characterize not diseases, but normalcy.

Maybe the reason that people are repulsed by madness is not simply because deception is destructive to individuals and societies; maybe people are horrified by its reality because madness highlights the fragile and deceptive nature of humanity. In this way, the false beliefs and fragility of others are like fine paintings that depict and reflect humanity's true nature. Pablo Picasso once said, "We all know that art is not truth. Art is a lie that makes us realize truth, at least the truth that is given us to understand."[413] In this way, madness has become an anthropological painting or mirror—a construct—which simply reflects the true ugly human condition which so many in society desire to deny and/or frame as abnormal. Yet today, much of society has accepted the evolutionary belief that posits madness as something "almost a species apart."[414]

THE BIBLICAL PERSPECTIVE

In contrast to the imprecise psychiatric perspective, the Bible consistently sets forth an anthropology that recognizes depravity (deception or moral failure) and fragility (impairment and weakness) to be at the core of human nature. Scripture also views madness as describing people's natural tendency to be overtaken with deception and not as a disorder. Mental fragility, false beliefs, their corresponding behaviors, and their destructive consequences are the foundational problems that all people face, and they are specific problems which Scripture addresses at length.

---

[414] Roy Porter, *Madness*, 185.

The biblical description of humanity is that people were created by God in his image and that they have both a material body and an immaterial soul. However, because of the rejection of God's truth by the first humans, Adam and Eve, human nature became incurably flawed and disordered with deceit and fragility. It is on this basis that the Bible asserts that the soul is by nature defective, and this defectiveness manifests itself in a myriad of areas. In this way people who exhibit symptoms of mental illness are not, according to biblical thinking, malfunctioning versions of their formerly functional selves; rather, they are simply exposing their humanity, their innate depravity/falsehood.

Though the idea of human depravity and fragility may seem, at first, to be a negative or unkind assessment of human struggle and madness, this view opens the door for empathy because it views all people as possessors of a soul and thus distinct from a machine or an animal. Dr. Peter Breggin explains how such a shift in thinking completely changes our approach to people's genuine mental struggles:

> If materialism is true in fully explaining human nature, then approaching people mechanistically without care of their souls makes logical sense. If people who express seemingly irrational ideas are best understood mechanistically, then these people are broken, disordered, or defective devices. If we take the viewpoint that they are persons, beings, or souls in struggle, then an infinite variety of more subtle possibilities comes to mind for understanding and helping those who seem mad, crazy, or deranged.[415]

When practitioners buy into the current view that humans are either functioning or mal-functioning organisms, the implications are frightening. Dr. Richard Bentall warns,

> Once we have decided that the patient's experiences are unintelligible, we are given an apparent license to treat the patient as a disordered

---

415 Breggin, *Toxic Psychiatry*, 25.

organism, a malfunctioning body that we do not have to relate to in a human way.[416]

As we observed in the previous chapter, history is replete with accounts which show the utter failure of attempting to treat the soul as if it were physical in nature or a bi-product of a biological mechanism. Furthermore, altruism does not make logical sense if people are only material beings. But what if the soul is considered once again to be distinct from the body and unapproachable with scientific tools? How would one go about seeking to change a person's false beliefs?

In construct to theories which view the soul through the lens of materialism, biblical counseling or "soul care" has been proven empirically to bring about positive results and provide healing to the soul/psyche. Though the cynic may deny that God created the world, reject the historical account of Genesis 3, and scoff at the idea of demons and an afterlife, he/she must still acknowledge the Bible's efficacy in helping people resolve their false beliefs. The clinician—no matter their worldview—who truly desires to help others rather than sustain his/her own beliefs should want to learn from this proven means of healing the soul. Though perhaps difficult for many modern theorists, Scripture offers a clear, simple, and consistent assessment of both madness and the condition of the soul.

In fact, the Bible offers one of the first clear descriptions of what psychiatrists today call psychosis. In Genesis 3:1-5, the Bible describes both original madness—where all of mankind became deceived—and its cause. The text first introduces the author of madness:

> Now the Serpent was craftier [having skill to achieve one's end by deceit; a scheme; manipulation] than any other beast of the field that the Lord God had made. He said to the woman, "Did God actually say, 'You shall not eat of any tree in the garden?'" And the woman said to the serpent, "We may eat of the fruit of the trees in the garden, but God said, "'You shall not eat of the fruit of the tree that is in the midst of the garden, neither shall you touch it, lest you die.'" But the serpent said to the woman, "You will not surely die. For God knows that when you

---

416 Ibid., 29.

> eat of it your eyes will be opened, and you will be like God, knowing good and evil."

There are several important elements of madness observed in this text. First of all, the origin of human madness is revealed to be the father of all lies: Satan, known also as the serpent or the great dragon. In Revelation 12:9, the Bible states that the "ancient serpent" is the Devil who deceives everyone:

> And the great dragon was thrown down, that ancient serpent, who is called the devil and Satan, the deceiver of the whole world—he was thrown down to the earth, and his angels were thrown down with him.

Of course, Satan is a spiritual being that cannot be observed, so materialists will be quick to dismiss his involvement in history as fact. But what if madness—false fixed beliefs—is sourced both in the work of the great deceiver and in humanity's original sin as Scripture declares? The historical account of Satan's involvement in deceit in the Garden of Eden does not suggest that psychosis/madness is equal to demon possession or oppression. It does, however, make clear that all human deception is born out of Satan's original scheme (to deceive the whole world) and is now naturally and deeply ingrained in the hearts of all people—a point that neuroscientists and neurologists who deny the validity and reliability of Scripture have also come to realize.

Though the Garden of Eden is where human madness began, the first recorded case of madness is observed in Satan's own history. Once again, the reader may wish to deny the historicity of the Bible, but its ancient depiction of madness/psychosis is precise and accurate—even from a psychiatric perspective. Isaiah 14:12-15 (a book of the Bible written several hundred years before Christ) declares,

> "How you are fallen from heaven, O Day Star, son of Dawn! How you are cut down to the ground, you who laid the nations low! You said in your heart, 'I will ascend to heaven; above the stars of God I will set my throne on high; I will sit on the mount of assembly in the far reaches of the north; I will ascend above the heights of the clouds; I will make myself like the Most High.' But you are brought down to Sheol, to the far reaches of the pit.

The first recorded state of psychosis is Satan's false belief that he was like God. As previously noted, modern psychiatrists call this way of thinking "grandiose delusions" "or delusions of grandeur" and insist that it is an abnormality:

> A *delusion of grandeur* is the fixed, false belief that one possesses superior qualities such as genius, fame, omnipotence, or wealth. It is most often a symptom of schizophrenia, but can also be a symptom found in psychotic or bipolar disorders.[417]

Not surprising, most delusions of grandeur have religious or supernatural themes as their primary content and often in relation to the Godhead:[418]

> Certain people may believe that they are a deity, sent from a deity to Earth with a special mission, or directly related to a deity. A common example is when people think that they are Jesus Christ.[419]

The APA defines this mindset as "a delusion of inflated worth, power, knowledge, identity or special relationship to a deity or famous person,"[420] and "believing that one is superior to others and deserves special treatment; self-centeredness; feelings of entitlement."[421] Many studies show that so-called normal people regularly experience delusions of grandeur,[422] and when pride dominates a person's character in observable ways, people are typically labeled as having something like "narcissistic

---

417 John M. Grohol, "Delusion of Grandeur," *Psych Central* 2016, https://psychcentral.com/encyclopedia/delusion-of-grandeur/.

418 "Delusions of Grandeur: Causes, Symptoms, and Treatment," http://mentalhealthdaily.com/2015/05/12/delusions-of-grandeur-causes-symptoms-treatment/.

419 Ibid.

420 APA, *DSM-5*, 819.

421 Ibid., 822.

422 Knowles, McCarthy-Jones, and Rowse, "Grandiose Delusions," 684-96.

personality disorder." [423] At this point the cynic may choose to dismiss such ideas as ridiculous, but there are too many similarities between the biblical accounts and the psychiatric concept of psychosis to overlook.

As previously discussed, *grandiose delusions* is a relatively new psychiatric term which describes pride and high self-esteem and that Scripture reveals to be the greatest deception, the cause of all deception, and a reflection of Satan's own character and original scheme. Obadiah 1:3a illustrates this reality: "The pride of your heart has deceived you." The text continues on to reference the fall of Satan. Pride (the false belief that one is greater than he/she is), whether observed in angels or humans, produces impairment and takes the participant further into deceit.

In Genesis 3, Satan promised Adam and Eve the same false claim that he himself believed: that they could be like God. Both Adam and Eve accepted this delusion and rejected God's truth. Romans 1 further explains that they, like everyone after them, chose in deceit to worship the creature rather than the Creator. The deceiver's crafty scheme had taken root in the human heart and made psychosis/delusional thinking/madness a core characteristic of all humanity.

It is also worth noting that deception began with Adam and Eve's false view of not only God but also themselves. Scripture presents all humanity as naturally having a false view of God and a wrong identity. Many of the psychiatric disorders in the *DSM-5* (e.g., personality disorders) attest to the fact that a person's identity is a common way in which people are deceived. "Borderline Personality Disorder" illustrates this point well. The *DSM-5* describes this construct as:

> The essential feature of borderline personality disorder is a pervasive pattern of instability of interpersonal relationships, self-image, and

---

423 "Delusions of Grandeur: Causes, Symptoms, and Treatment," http://mentalhealthdaily.com/2015/05/12/delusions-of-grandeur-causes-symptoms-treatment/.

> affects, and marked impulsivity that begins by early adulthood and is present in a variety of contexts.[424]

Or take as another example "Avoidant Personality Disorder,"

> The essential feature of avoidant personality disorder is a pervasive pattern of social inhibition, feelings of inadequacy, and hypersensitivity to negative evaluation that begins by early adulthood and is present in a variety of contexts . . . . These individuals avoid making new friends unless they are certain they will be liked and accepted without criticism.[425]

Other criteria in constructs such as depression expose the same underlying deceit: "Feelings of worthlessness" and "self-derogatory ideation."[426] Viewing oneself in truth rather than falsehood is essential to remedy madness, and it is a starting point that Scripture addresses at length. In other words, having an accurate anthropology is important both to form a definition of madness as well as to remedy insanity.

The Bible stresses that the deception which occurred in the garden is not unique to Adam and Eve. Though he is not seen, and his schemes are well-disguised, Satan is actively deceiving the entire world. John 8:44 remarks,

> You are of your father the devil, and your will is to do your father's desires. He was a murderer from the beginning, and has nothing to do with truth, because there is no truth in him. When he lies, he speaks out of his own character, for he is a liar and the father of lies.

Not only is Satan the source of what is false, he is diametrically opposed to truth. This text also exposes how madness is recognized: through one's words. When Satan speaks, his deceived nature becomes evident. Likewise, as John 8:44 indicates, when a person embraces deceit, he/she will act accordingly. It is also worth reiterating that madness in Scripture is not always attributed to demonic activity as many historians

---

[424] APA, *DSM-5*, 663.

[425] Ibid., 673.

[426] Ibid., 161.

portray it to be. They are often related because of the nature of falsehood, but not all deception is demonic oppression or possession; since the fall, the human psyche has been naturally deceived above all other things on its own. What is also clear in the Bible is that both pride and deception (false fixed beliefs)—no matter how deep and impairing—reflect the mind of Satan, and the commonality of being deceived is ultimately sourced in the great deceiver.

The Bible not only explains where madness originated, but it also stresses that deception is universal and the source of humanity's greatest problems. Revelation 12:9 as well as other passages expose that Satan is "the deceiver of the whole world." Since the fall of Adam and Eve in the Garden of Eden, all humanity is born into deception and must pursue finding spiritual truth and discovering natural truth. In reality, even if a person denies this historical fact, they must still concede that all humanity is burdened with impairing deceit and seek to understand why and where this impairment began.

Scripture emphasizes throughout that both pride and deception are not abnormalities; they are shared characteristics of all humanity after the fall. Jeremiah 17:9 states, "The heart [soul] is deceitful above all things, and desperately sick; who can understand it?" The phrase "desperately sick" in Hebrew literally means "incurably sick"; the minds/psyches/spiritual hearts of all people are sick with unimaginable deceit. Nothing in this world compares to the deception found in the human heart, and, apart from God's truth, nothing in this world can remedy it either. In fact, Genesis 3 establishes that physical death and the hopeless condition of all humanity are directly related to humanity corporately falling into deceit; truly, we are deeply deceived in a way that leaves us hopeless apart from absolute moral truth.

In Romans 6:23, the Bible explains further that because of sin (perversion of truth; e.g., stealing instead of working or hating instead of loving) death is inevitable: "The wages of sin is death." What perverting truth pays out is killing of both the soul and body. Every person, because of deceit, will face death, and in order to be healed, a person's faith must fundamentally change from falsehood to truth. Such a change will also transform a person's behavior.

What is also noteworthy in Jeremiah 17:9-10 is that the spiritual heart/psyche is identified in Scripture as being a mystery to humanity. According to these verses and others, the scientific process cannot reveal truths about the spiritual heart/soul, and only God is able to observe and measure the psyche—a point which was established in chapter four. This reality makes theology, discernment, and faith vital to establishing what is morally true and what is false and vital to remedy the soul.

The theological term regularly used in Scripture for those who naturally lack God's wisdom/moral truth and live according to their deceitful hearts is "foolish" or "fools." However, foolishness is the term which describes normalcy and not a group of people who are set aside as abnormal; the natural mind is by nature blinded to spiritual truths. Proverbs 22:15a states, "Folly is bound up in the heart of a child." First Corinthians 2:12-16 also says:

> Now we have received not the spirit of the world, but the spirit who is from God, that we might understand the things freely given us by God. And we impart this in words not taught by human wisdom but taught by the spirit, interpreting spiritual truths to those who are spiritual. The natural person [normal human nature] does not accept the things of the Spirit of God, for they are folly [madness] to him, and he is not able to understand them because they are spiritually discerned.

There are vital moral truths that the natural soul apart from God's grace cannot understand or believe; he/she is incurably sick with deception. This is the natural spiritual blindness of all humanity, and it is clear evidence that Satan is deceiving the whole world. Madness, then, defines all people's natural inability apart from Christ to receive spiritual truth despite the physical evidence available. In this sense, all humanity is disordered when compared to Christ in whom there is found no deceit.

Those who have received the truth of Jesus Christ, though, still have a depraved nature that can be deceived. Colossians 2:8 admonishes, "See to it that no one takes you captive by philosophy and empty deceit, according to the elemental spirits of the world [the original scheme of the devil from Genesis 3], and not according to Christ [His plan of redemption and deliverance]." While believers still have a deceived nature that they must continually confront, their faith rests in God's truth that is supernaturally able to restore the soul and is progressively doing so.

Though the Bible discusses madness, provides records of people who judged others to be mad, and reveals the foundational aspects of madness to be faith and falsehood, Scripture does not differentiate between those who are mad and those who are not. The reason is simple: Scripture sees all humanity as naturally being depraved, deceived, weak, and dependent upon faith. Madness in Scripture is used as an identifier of one who has embraced or has been given over to deception rather than as a category of human abnormalities. This right view of mankind does not stigmatize some people with the concept of madness. Instead, the Bible makes it clear that all humanity possesses the same destructive nature: a soul or psyche that is fragile, deceived above all known things, and incurably sick apart from faith in Jesus Christ.

The Remedy for the Human Soul

As seen throughout this book, madness is a condition of the soul which amounts to false beliefs and/or perceptions that are invisible but which produce impairing-observable behavior. Because the core discussion of madness is about the condition of the soul, the immaterial nature of mankind, faith, deception, and outworking behavior, Scripture must be considered as these are all major themes throughout its pages.

Discovering the true nature of madness also allows people to better understand why madness and the human psyche were first treated under the care of the pastor and church members with great success. In fact, biblical counselors today are still seeing the Bible positively transform lives out of the deepest and most dominating false beliefs.

While the modern reader may be tempted to view the Bible as an ancient, out-of-touch religious book, its assessment of humanity (that we are all in need of rescue) fits with scientific conclusions about mental illness: biological disease is not the culprit -- we all are the culprits, and if we are honest with ourselves, we know it. At first glance, many view the Bible's perspective as harsh, but it, unlike the pharmaceutical and psychiatric industries, does not stigmatize a few. Rather, Scripture freely offers all of us hope for deep healing and restoration. God designed Scripture to reveal Himself, to reveal true human nature, and to remedy madness—putting off falsehood and restoring the soul/psyche to spiritual health or righteousness.

The Bible also offers specific counsel on how to endure trauma and other difficult experiences, and it explains how people's ability to endure trauma or hardship is directly linked to their faith. James 1:3-8, as one illustration, declares,

> Count it all joy, my brothers, when you meet trials [evil experiences, traumas, or hardships] of various kinds, for you know that the testing of your faith produces steadfastness. And let steadfastness have its full effect, that you may be perfect and complete, lacking in nothing. If any of you lacks wisdom, let him ask God, who gives generously to all without reproach, and it will be given him. But let him ask in faith, with no doubting, for the one who doubts is like a wave of the sea that is driven and tossed by the wind. For that person must not suppose that he will receive anything from the Lord; he is a double-minded man, unstable in all his ways.

Faith in God's truth/perspective is essential to endure trials of various kinds and have a sound mind. Likewise, 1 Peter 1:6-7 states:

> In this you rejoice, though now for a little while, if necessary, you have been grieved by various trials, so that the tested genuineness of your faith—more precious than gold that perishes though it is tested by fire—may be found to result in praise and glory and honor at the revelation of Jesus Christ.

Trials or trauma test the validity and reliability of a person's faith, and faith that cannot explain or provide endurance through hardship is not reliable; it is false fixed belief which can easily lead to further deceit and distress. Everyone responds to trials according to faith (i.e., a belief system). If this foundational faith is tested, shown to be false, but still kept, it will reveal itself in deeper false mindsets and observable-impairing behavior.

The Bible is so precise and profitable that it is able to explain people who have embraced the deepest deception and to remedy their hearts with sound faith. The Bible, unlike psychotherapies, however, contains eternal truth that not only remedies the mind but resolves such issues as hopelessness, guilt, identity, fear, sorrow, and life after death. Scripture's ability to remedy the human soul is founded on the basis that One exists who has never been deceived, who provides a standard of what is truth, who exemplifies a faith that can endure severe trauma, who is the object of faith and hope that people need to be restored, and who took upon Himself our guilt, perversions/transgressions, condemnation, and sorrow. That person is Jesus Christ:

> [Christ] committed no sin, neither was deceit found in his mouth. When he was reviled he did not revile in return; when he suffered, he did not threaten, but continued entrusting himself to him who judges justly. He himself bore our sins in his body on the tree, that we might die to sin and live to righteousness. By his wounds you have been healed. For you were straying like sheep, but have now returned to the Shepherd and Overseer of your souls (1 Peter 2:22-25).

Because no perversion or deceit is in Christ, He is able to be the overseer of people's psyches/souls, restore them to His likeness, and change them from Satan's likeness. This is precisely why Christ is called the truth (John 14:6), and He is able to cure the most deceitful "condition of the soul" (psychosis). It is likewise important to note that Jesus provides not only the remedy but also a standard of normalcy; He is the truth to which our souls need to be restored; He is the great physician as well as the standard of mental health. In comparison to his mind, every human is disordered and in need of restoration.

Having an accurate understanding of human nature enables one to have an accurate and objective definition of madness. Likewise, a right anthropology enables a right understanding of causation and provides a proven remedy. People must choose to believe that all humanity is deceived in a destructive way or believe that just some people are. They must choose to believe that faith is caused by a physical malfunction or that faith is a spiritual condition of everyone's soul as a person relates to spiritual truth. Whichever belief one chooses, his/her belief about normalcy will ultimately determine his/her definition of madness and the subsequent theories.

If falsehood (depravity) is the underlying problem of humanity, then spiritual truth found in Scripture provides the only genuine remedy to enable right faith. The Bible has for centuries provided a tried and true moral system which differentiates healthy mindsets and behaviors from those which are deceitful and destructive. Likewise, the Bible does not simply delineate between truth and falsehood, it provides the means to restore the soul to complete health (Psalm 19:4-6). The New Testament expounds on this claim further. For instance, in 2 Peter 1:1-9, Peter reminds those who share the same faith in Christ (1-2) that God has given believers everything they need for life (including hardships) and to have their souls restored to His divine likeness:

> His divine power has granted to us all things that pertain to life and godliness, through the knowledge of him who called us to his own glory and excellence, by which he has granted to us his precious and very great promises, so that through them you may become partakers of the divine nature, having escaped from the corruption that is in the world because of sinful desire (verses 3-4).

Peter then reiterates that faith in God's truth is the foundation on which character, wisdom, self-control, endurance, restoration/healing, and love for others is built:

> For this very reason, make every effort to supplement your faith with virtue, and virtue with knowledge, and knowledge with self-control, and self-control with steadfastness, and steadfastness with godliness, and godliness with brotherly affection, and brotherly affection with

love. For if these qualities are yours and increasing, they keep you from being ineffective or unfruitful in the knowledge of our Lord Jesus Christ (verses 5-8).

In other words, faith in Jesus Christ enables positive character and produces right behavior. But the text also warns Christians to be aware of their own spiritual blindness (madness): "For whoever lacks these qualities is so nearsighted that he is blind, having forgotten that he was cleansed from his former sins" (9). It is important to note here that the blindness (being deceived) pertains to the person's history, own anthropology, and highlights natural pride. One who is walking in God's truth recognizes that he/she has been delivered from walking in deceit, yet when one forgets his/her true condition, he/she will resort back to his/her natural tendency of pride. Truly, to remedy madness must begin with having a biblical (truthful) view of self in relation to God.

The Bible claims that its message is restorative; healing faith only comes from hearing the immutable truth contained in the Word of God. While the Bible's claim to restore the soul from deceit is sufficient for Christians to believe, the skeptic desires empirical evidence. Fortunately, such evidence is available. Scientific studies consistently show that biblical counseling yields positive results and can change people's delusions. In fact, there are numerous studies that show how biblical counseling[427] produces better outcomes in counselees than does secular counseling. For example, former president of the American Psychology Association John Norcross helped author a book in which numerous independent controlled studies were reviewed—each revealing that "Christian therapy" was more effective in changing beliefs and in treating depression than was secular or "non-religious therapy."[428] The studies, which utilized

---

427 The study defined a "Christian therapist" as a person who used: "Christian beliefs to dispute irrational beliefs, encouraged the use of Christian imagery homework, and utilized brief prayer in sessions" (Norcross, Worthington, and Sandage, *Psychotherapy Relationships That Work*, 391-92).

428 Ibid., 391-92.

various forms of counseling/therapy approaches, specifically showed that offering "Bible verses or religious themes of interest to the clients" could positively change their false beliefs: "Christian RET [rational-emotive therapy] was also effective in reducing client's irrational beliefs (but standard [non-religious] RET was not."[429] The same was true with cognitive-behavioral forms of counseling (CBT) and counseling that focuses on a person's identity (PCT):

> "Clients in both religious CBT and PCT [person-centered therapy; where the counselee's religious beliefs are important factors in counseling] reported significantly lower post-treatment depression and better social adjustment than did clients in either the nonreligious CBT or WLC [wait list control group] conditions."[430]

What is also worth noting from one study is that even when non-Christian therapists implemented Scripture and theological content into their sessions—as their Christian counterparts had done—the outcomes were also noticeably better than the same counselor's secular approach.[431] Such evidence indicates that the Bible is powerful; it can help people's minds to positively change even when the person offering its truths does not believe in it.

While biblical counselors regularly see counselees positively changing, positive beliefs (faith in truth) is not something that a counselor can force upon anyone; the hearer must accept God's truths in order for saving faith and lasting change to occur. Positive life changes which occur in counselees' lives, then, are not the result of the biblical counselor's expertise or delivery, but are the result of the power of the gospel which is able to positively change the condition of the soul. Faith that can restore the soul comes "from hearing and hearing from the Word of God" (Romans 10:17).

---

429 Ibid., 392.

430 Ibid.

431 Ibid.

CONCLUSION

False fixed beliefs are not anomalies or abnormalities; they are foundational to human nature. Likewise, human distress and impairment are not diseases; they are a part of what it means to be normal. In this way, the construct of mental illnesses has become a means of sustaining the evolutionary theory of man—an exception clause to support a wrong anthropology.

As with the individuals in Scripture who rejected the prophet's truth and labeled the messenger as mad, those who are content to label some as mad are often themselves the most deceived. Instead of believing the true nature of humanity, many are content to set aside those whom they view as being the most deceived in order to sustain their own false beliefs. Maybe in part, the reason that prominent secular theorists have not arrived at an objective definition of madness or mental illness is that they have failed to recognize or have outright denied that false fixed beliefs are a shared normal human condition.

Rather than accepting the objective definition of madness to simply describe a person who has embraced false beliefs, psychiatric theorists have attempted to transform it into a disease entity in order to maintain and protect a false view of humanity, sustain social control and their own existence, and keep falsehood and faith—the core elements of madness—from being considered matters of religion and remedied with truth. By refusing to offer an objective and precise definition of madness, secular theorists can continue disguising their own false fixed beliefs about humanity. But such a position serves to stigmatize some of those who need truth and leads society into further insanity.

In contrast to secular theories of normalcy and madness, the Bible offers a clear unchanging understanding of humanity, which teaches that all people are by nature deeply deceived, impaired, frail, and hopeless apart from Christ. It offers not only clear definitions but also truth about the one, Jesus Christ, who is without deceit and is able to fully restore the soul to spiritual health by addressing false beliefs and offering saving faith.

CHAPTER 7

CONCLUSION

"Much of what is practiced in the tradition of psychodynamic psychotherapy, and often paid for collectively as mental health care, is little more than modern mesmerism. Its power comes not from truth telling but from belief building."[432]
Ethan Watters and Richard Ofshe, journalists

"For the past fifty years in the United States and Canada, psychologists have been building fences, charging fees, making laws and padlocking their turf; all in an attempt to claim their role as keepers of psychological knowledge and to establish themselves as the legitimate dispensers of psychological wisdom and healing. Where they can, they have subverted basic truth into egocentric possessions; and where they can't, they have manufactured truths to expand their activities and to maximize their profits."[433]
Tana Dineen, psychologist

Throughout history *madness* has had an objective and consistent definition. Whether it is in the ancient record of the Bible or in the modern *DSM-5*, at its core, *insanity* has always been a term that describes a person given over to deceit, whose beliefs and perceptions were found to be false, or someone who turned to falsehood in attempt to deal with trauma, hardship, or guilt. False beliefs are clearly the essential feature of historical madness.

---

[432] Watters and Ofshe, *Therapy's Delusions*, 27.

[433] Dineen, *Manufacturing Victims*, 12.

While today's secular theory of mental illness (neo-Kraepelinianism) reflects the historical definition, psychiatrists have altered the meaning of *madness* in attempt to explain mindsets and behaviors which fall outside of their imprecise view of normalcy. In essence, they have attempted to turn false beliefs and their outworking behavior as well as common human weaknesses into abnormalities by categorizing them as disorders. All mental illnesses contained in the *DSM-5* are either specific false fixed belief, common human impairment that is falsely believed to be abnormalities, or neurodegenerative syndromes that were once called idiocy and should not be primarily considered as mental illness or problems in thinking.

Much of modern society has accepted the psychiatric perspective, yet this view denies that mental illness or normality can even be defined objectively. Psychiatrists have convinced many of their speculative theory by insisting on a materialistic and humanistic view of mankind, providing new nomenclature for common impairing mindsets and behavior, speculating with unabashed faith about biological causes, and insisting that a person's false beliefs can be changed by physical means.

In the process of denying an objective definition of madness, modern theorists have introduced the insanity of madness: they have rejected or ignored the true nature of madness, denied essential absolute truths, and constructed a theory built upon a false anthropology, which is incapable of explaining the human mind and behaviors or even defining normalcy. They have asserted these theories without an objective definition of mental illness, while at the same time, insisting that society in general view faith and falsehood as primarily biological and medical problems without providing supportive empirical evidence. Of course, the claim that empirical evidence and a big breakthrough are just around the corner has sustained the belief in materialism for decades. But secularists' confession that they cannot objectively define normalcy or alleged abnormalities exposes that they do not understand what it truly means to be human.

Still they continue to assert that they are the authority over understanding what causes and what remedies the mind.

But until a precise objective definition of mental illness exists, one cannot logically claim to understand what it is, where it comes from, and how it is remedied. Rather than focusing their attention on what constitutes mental illness, many secular researchers and clinicians are enthusiastic about proving their theories of etiology and promoting their alleged mechanisms for healing—all of which continue to fail. In essence, these theorists do not know what it is, but they are somehow sure what causes and remedies it. Instead of accepting that false belief is the very essence of madness throughout history and the core of the Kraepelinian construct of mental illness today, most clinicians are content to focus on and even suppress behavior while ignoring how vital one's acceptance of truth is in order to restore the human soul.

It is only when a person understands and accepts the objective historical definition of madness that a clear cause and remedy for mental illness can be understood. If false beliefs are destructive and make the body unhealthy, then logically, a person's acceptance of truth can set his/her soul free and remedy physical symptoms. Turning from falsehood to truth, then, must be the focus of all remedies for false fixed beliefs and false perceptions. It is not people that change another person's beliefs, however, but truth. People are merely conduits of truth or falsehood in how they relate to others.

Researchers and psychiatric theorists have not discovered diseases of the mind or advanced the healing of the soul; they have simply taken common, ongoing, and impairing mindsets and behaviors, grouped them together, and imposed onto them labels and humanistic ways of interpretation. Despite their countless attempts to use biological and medical means to remedy madness, it remains outside of their ability to heal.

Because of the difficulty of modern psychiatry to provide definitions and answers, it is worthwhile to examine traditional, biblical explanations for human struggle. In fact, as previously discussed throughout this book and recognized by most historians, the best historical record of madness is found in the Bible. Could the cause and remedy also rest in the pages of Scripture where a clear objective definition exists and is still relevant today? The psychiatric construct of mental illness is not a different topic from madness; insanity has simply been reframed within a medical perspective. Could it be that ancient immutable truth rather than modern medicine has answers to false beliefs overlooked by a society enamored with and trusting in scientific solutions?

Only God's reliable moral truth can solve the riddle that is madness, and more importantly, only God's wisdom can remedy the deceived and impaired hearts of humanity. These answers do not come in a ritual or in a religion; rather help comes through a relationship with the only true God by means of faith (John 3:26; 17:3). It is through knowing the true God that deceived people can find all answers that pertain to their souls, and correct false beliefs and destructive behavior (2 Peter 1:1-3).

Ultimately, the insanity of madness is to accept the greatest and most destructive delusion which denies God as Creator and worships mankind instead (Romans 1:18-23; 29):

> For the wrath of God is revealed from heaven against all ungodliness and unrighteousness of men, who by their unrighteousness suppress the truth [*false fixed belief*]. For what can be known about God is plain to them, because God has shown it to them. For his invisible attributes, namely, his eternal power and divine nature, have been clearly perceived, ever since the creation of the world, in the things that have been made [*despite clear irrefutable evidence*]. So they are without excuse. For although they knew God, they did not honor him as God or give thanks to him, but they became futile in their thinking, and their foolish hearts were darkened [*deeper into madness*]. Claiming to be wise, they became fools, and exchanged the glory of the immortal God for images resembling mortal man and birds and animals and creeping things. . . . They are full of envy, murder, strife, deceit, maliciousness.

Having a truthful view of human nature is essential to remedy the mind and its destructive behavior. Without objective truth there exists no madness, and without the truth of Jesus Christ and His atoning work on the cross, there exists no lasting means of escaping the destructive nature of deceit.

The Bible provides an objective definition of madness, a precise standard of normalcy, a clear unchanging perspective of humanity that does not stigmatize some, a consistent etiological explanation, and a reliable, proven, and timeless remedy for madness. The message of Jesus Christ is consistently transforming people's lives from every mindset, emotion, and behavior that psychiatrists have framed as mental illness. As observed, there exists a great amount of empirical evidence available—conducted by secular researchers—that should make any counselor or clinician who genuinely wants to help others through mental turmoil consider why such faith is so positively transformational.[434]

People long for help for their diagnoses of mental illness. The remedy, as with the definition of mental illness, is too often hidden by much speculation and endless hypotheses. Yet, the remedy lies ready to heal the soul's terminal condition; it is simply truth. If madness is complete confidence in falsehood, then sanity is a full embrace of God's truth that transforms thinking and behavior throughout a person's life. Accepting this truth requires accepting that each of us are incurably deceived, intrinsically flawed, incredibly frail and dying, and unable to be restored through material/pharmaceutical means or human effort apart from faith in Christ. The simplicity of the ancient biblical solution indicates that we must look to God in faith for our help. This divine solution is the ultimate embrace of reality because it demands an honest evaluation of our impaired human condition and our need for salvation, and it offers the ultimate solution to heal the madness of the human soul.

---

434 Norcross, Worthington, and Sandage, *Psychotherapy Relationships That Work*, 384-92.

BIBLIOGRAPHY

Akiskal, Hagop S., and William T. McKinney, Jr. "Psychiatry and Pseudopsychiatry." *Archives of General Psychiatry* 28 (1973): 367-73.

American Psychiatric Association. *Diagnostic and Statistical Manual of Mental Disorders*. 5th ed. Washington, DC: American Psychiatric Publishing, 2013.

———. *Diagnostic Criteria from the DSM-IV-TR*. Washington, D.C.: American Psychiatric Association, 2000.

———. "Euthanasia." *American Journal of Psychiatry* 99 (1942): 141-43.

American Psychiatric Publishing Textbook of Forensic Psychiatry. Edited by Robert Simon and Lisa Gold. Washington, D.C.: American Psychiatric Publishing, 2010.

Beer, M. Dominic. "Psychosis: From Mental Disorder to Disease Concept." *History of Psychiatry* 6, no. 22 (June 1, 1995): 177–200.

Bentall, Richard. *Madness Explained: Psychosis and Human Nature*. New York: Penguin, 2003.

Berger II, Daniel. *Mental Illness: The Influence of Nurture*. Taylors, SC: Alethia International Publications, 2016.

______. *Mental Illness: The Necessity for Dependence*. Taylors, SC: Alethia International Publications, 2016.

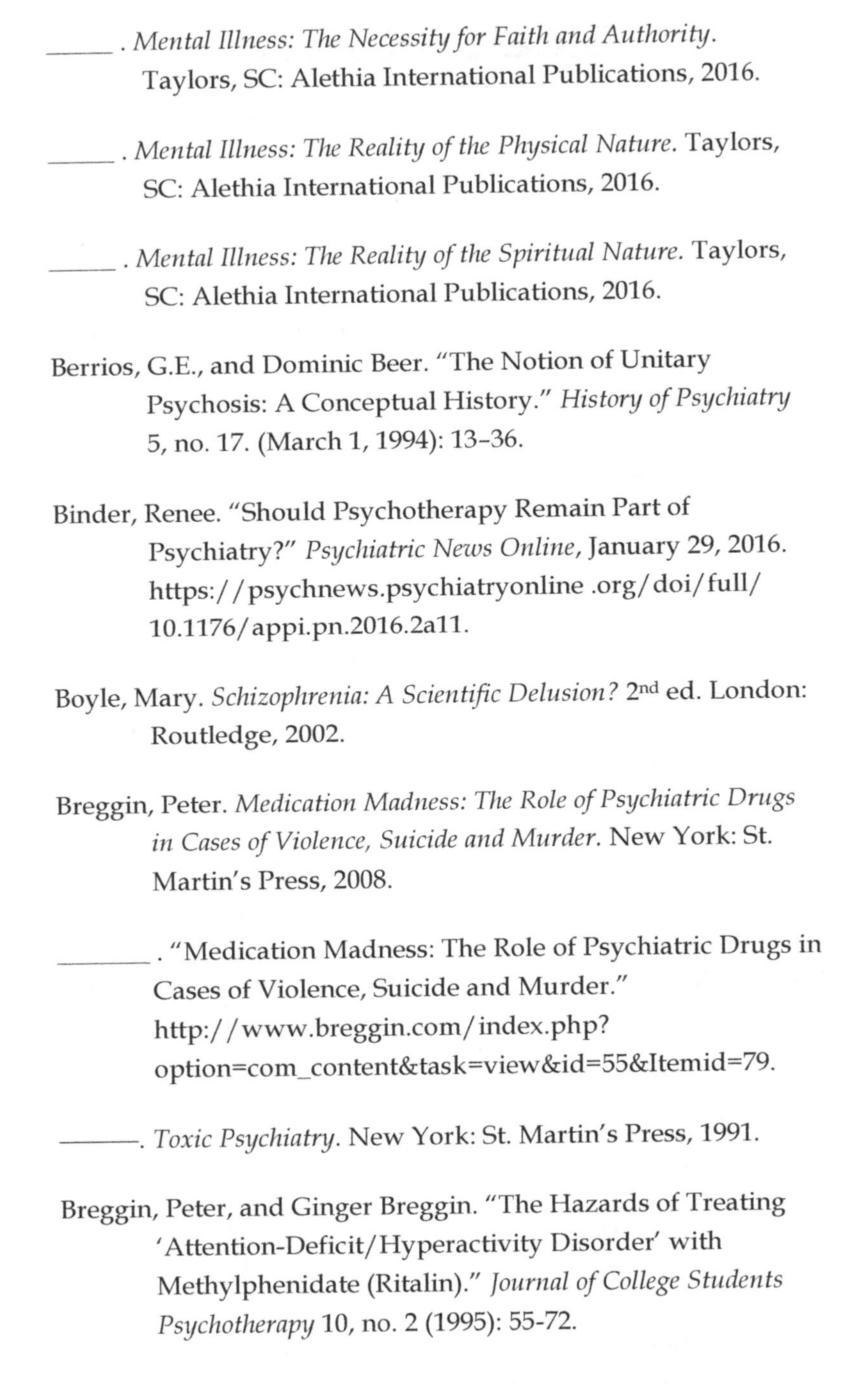

_____ . *Mental Illness: The Necessity for Faith and Authority*. Taylors, SC: Alethia International Publications, 2016.

_____ . *Mental Illness: The Reality of the Physical Nature*. Taylors, SC: Alethia International Publications, 2016.

_____ . *Mental Illness: The Reality of the Spiritual Nature*. Taylors, SC: Alethia International Publications, 2016.

Berrios, G.E., and Dominic Beer. "The Notion of Unitary Psychosis: A Conceptual History." *History of Psychiatry* 5, no. 17. (March 1, 1994): 13–36.

Binder, Renee. "Should Psychotherapy Remain Part of Psychiatry?" *Psychiatric News Online*, January 29, 2016. https://psychnews.psychiatryonline .org/doi/full/10.1176/appi.pn.2016.2a11.

Boyle, Mary. *Schizophrenia: A Scientific Delusion?* 2nd ed. London: Routledge, 2002.

Breggin, Peter. *Medication Madness: The Role of Psychiatric Drugs in Cases of Violence, Suicide and Murder*. New York: St. Martin's Press, 2008.

_______ . "Medication Madness: The Role of Psychiatric Drugs in Cases of Violence, Suicide and Murder." http://www.breggin.com/index.php?option=com_content&task=view&id=55&Itemid=79.

———. *Toxic Psychiatry*. New York: St. Martin's Press, 1991.

Breggin, Peter, and Ginger Breggin. "The Hazards of Treating 'Attention-Deficit/Hyperactivity Disorder' with Methylphenidate (Ritalin)." *Journal of College Students Psychotherapy* 10, no. 2 (1995): 55-72.

Brooks, Samantha J., and Dan J. Stein. "A Systematic Review of the Neural Bases of Psychotherapy for Anxiety and related disorders." *Dialogues in Clinical Neuroscience* 3 (September 17, 2015): 261-79.

Chesterton, Gilbert K. *Orthodoxy*. London: John Lane, 1908. http://www.freeclassice books.com/Chesterton,%20 G.%20K/Orthodoxy.pdf.

Chisholm, G. Brock. *Psychiatry: Journal of Biology and Pathology of Interpersonal Relations* 9, no. 1 (February 1946).

Crick, Francis. *The Astonishing Hypothesis: The Scientific Search for the Soul*. New York: Simon and Schuster, 1995.

Dineen, Tana. *Manufacturing Victims: What the Psychology Industry is Doing to People*, 3rd ed. New York: Robert Davies Multimedia Publishing, 2000.

Eagleman, David. *The Brain: The Story of You*. New York: Pantheon Books, 2015.

Ebert, Andreas, and Karl-Jürgen Bär. "Emil Kraepelin: A Pioneer of Scientific Understanding of Psychiatry and Psychopharmacology." *Indian Journal of Psychiatry* 52, no. 2 (Apr-Jun 2010): 191-92.

Eiss, Harry. *Insanity and Genius: Masks of Madness and the Mapping of Meaning and Value*, 2nd ed. New Castle, England: Cambridge Scholars Publishing, 2008.

English Standard Version. Wheaton: Good News, 2001.

Engstrom, E.J., and K.S. Kendler. "Emil Kraepelin: Icon and Reality." *American Journal of Psychiatry* 172, no. 12 (December 1, 2015): 1190-96. https://doi.org/10.1176/appi.ajp.2015.15050665.

Frances, Allen. "Reconciling, Recovery, and Psychiatry: Response to Open Letter, Finding the Right Balance." *Psychology Today Online*, September 15, 2013. https://www.psychologytoday.com/blog/saving-normal/201309/reconciling-recovery-and-psychiatry-response-open-letter.

———. *Saving Normal: An Insider's Revolt against Out-of-Control Psychiatric Diagnosis, DSM-5, Big Pharma, and the Medicalization of Ordinary Life*. New York: HarperCollins, 2013.

Frank, Jerome. *Persuasion and Healing: A Comparative Study of Psychotherapy*. 1st ed. Baltimore: Johns Hopkins University Press, 1961.

Frankl, Viktor E. *Man's Search for Meaning*. Boston: Beacon Press, 2006.

Freud, Sigmund. "Postscript to the Question of Lay Analysis," *SE* 20 (1927): 255-56.

"Gender Ideology Harms Children." *American College of Pediatrics Online,* January 2017. https://www.acpeds.org/the-college-speaks/position-statements/gender-ideology-harms-children.

Ghanbari Jolfaei, Atefeh, Mehdi Nasr Isfahani, and Reza Bidaki. "Folie À Deux and Delusional Disorder by Proxy in a Family." *Journal of Research in Medical Sciences: The Official Journal of Isfahan University of Medical Sciences* 16, no. 1 (2011): S453–S455.

Goodwin, F.K., and K.R.Jamison. *Manic-Depressive Illness: Bipolar Disorders and Recurrent Depression*. Oxford: Oxford University Press, 1990.

Greenberg, Gary. "Inside the Battle to Define Mental Illness." *Wired Magazine Online*, December 27, 2010. https://www.wired.com/2010/12/ff_dsmv/.

———. *The Book of Woe: The DSM and the Unmaking of Psychiatry*. New York: Blue Rider Press, 2013.

Grohol, John M. "Delusion of Grandeur." *Psych Central*, 2016. https://psychcentral.com/encyclopedia/delusion-of-grandeur/.

Group for the Advancement of Psychiatry. "History of Psychiatry 19th Century." YouTube video, 31.45. Posted May 3, 2015. https://m.youtube.com/watch?feature=youtu. be&v=TFoJ0b4v3hY: 18:45-55.

Healy, David. *Let Them Eat Prozac: The Unhealthy Relationship between the Pharmaceutical Industry and Depression*. New York: New York University Press, 2004.

Holmes, Sr., Oliver Wendell. *Autocrat of the Breakfast Table*. 1858. Reprint, New York: Cosimo, 2005.

Hubble, Mark, Barry Duncan, and Scott Miller. *The Heart and Soul of Change: What Works in Therapy*. Washington, D.C.: American Psychological Association, 1999.

Jung, Carl G. *The Integration of the Personality*. Translated by Stanley Dell. New York: Farrar & Rinehart Inc., 1939.

Kagan, Jerome. "What about Tutoring Instead of Pills?" *Spiegel Online*, August 2, 2012. http://www.spiegel.de/international/world/child-psychologist-jerome-kagan-on-overprescibing-drugs-to-children-a-847500.html.

Kandel, Eric. *In Search of Memory: The Emergence of a New Science of Mind*. New York: Norton Publishing Company, 2006.

———. *Psychiatry, Psychoanalysis, and the New Biology of Mind.* Arlington, VA: American Psychiatric Publishing, 2005.

Kendell, R. E. *The Role of Diagnosis in Psychiatry*. Oxford: Blackwell, 1975.

Knowles, R., S. McCarthy-Jones, and G. Rowse. "Grandiose Delusions: A Review and Theoretical Integration of Cognitive and Affective Perspectives." *Clinical Psychology Review* 4 (June 31, 2011): 684-96.

Kraepelin, Emil. "Clinical Manifestations of Mental Illness," *History of Psychiatry* 3 (1920): 499-529.

———. "Die Erscheinungsformen des Irreseins," *Zeitschrift fur die gesamte Neurologie und Psychiatrie* 62 (1920), 27.

———. *Manic Depressive Insanity and Paranoia* (*Dementia Praecox and Paraphrenia*). Translated by Mary Barclay. Edinburgh: E. and S. Livingstone, 1921.

———. *Psychiatrie*, 6th ed. Leipzig: Barth, 1899.

Kutchins, Herb, and Stuart A. Kirk. *Making Us Crazy: DSM: The Psychiatric Bible and the Creation of Mental Disorders*. New York: Free Press, 1997.

Lanczik, M. "Heinrich Neumann und seine Lehre von der Einheitspsychose." *Fundamenta Psychaitrica* 3 (1989): 49-54.

Lee, Allison, Igor Galynker, Irina Kopeykina, Hae-Joon Kim, and Tasnia Khatun. "Violence in Bipolar Disorder." *Psychiatric Times Online*, December 16, 2014. http://www.psychiatrictimes.com/bipolar-disorder/violence-bipolar-disorder?GUID=31158D64-F01A-4DEA-AC1A-D3CE843FC9BC&rememberme=1&ts=21042017.

Lewontin, Richard C. "Billions and Billions of Demons." Review of *The Demon-Haunted World: Science as a Candle in the Dark*, by Carl Sagan. *New York Review of Books*, January 7, 1997.

Lieberman, Jeffrey A. *Shrinks: The Untold Story of Psychiatry*. New York: Little, Brown and Company, 2015.

Lifton, Robert Jay. *The Nazi Doctors: Medical Killing and the Psychology of Genocide*. New York: Basic Books, 1986.

Menninger, Karl. *The Vital Balance: The Life Process in Mental Health and Illness*. New York: Viking Press, 1968.

Micale, Mark, and Roy Porter, eds. *Discovering the History of Psychiatry*. New York: Oxford University Press, 1994.

Murray, Evan D., Miles G. Cunningham, and Bruce H. Price. "The Role of Psychotic Disorders in Religious History Considered." *Journal of Neuropsychiatry and Clinical Neurosciences* 24 (2012): 410-26.

Murray, Robin M. "Mistakes I Have Made in My Research Career." *Schizophrenia Bulletin Online*, December 2016. sbw165. doi: 10.1093/schbul/sbw165.

Norcross, John, Everett L. Worthington, Jr., and Steven J. Sandage. *Psychotherapy Relationships That Work: Therapist Contributions and Responsiveness to Patients*. New York: Oxford University Press, 2002.

Panksepp, Jaak, ed. *Textbook of Biological Psychiatry*. New York: John Wiley and Sons, 2004.

Parnask, Josef, Louis A.Sass, and Dan Zahavi. "Rediscovering Psychopathology: The Epistemology and Phenomenology of the Psychiatric Object." *Schizophrenia Bulletin* 39, no. 2 (2013): 270-77.

Patel, Vikram, Alistair Woodward, Valery L. Feigin, Kristian Heggenhougen, and Stella R. Quah, eds. *Mental and Neurological Public Health: A Global Perspective*. San Diego: Academic Press, 2010.

Pert, Candace B. *Molecules of Emotion: The Science behind Mind-Body Medicine*. New York: Scribner, 1997.

Pettus, Ashley. "Psychiatry by Prescription: Do Psychotropic Drugs Blur the Boundaries between Illness and Health?" *Harvard Magazine Online*, July-August, 2006. http://harvardmagazine.com/2006/07/psychiatry-by-prescripti.html.

Pies, Ronald. "Hearing Voices and Psychiatry's (Real) Medical Model." *Psychiatric Times Online*, September 4, 2017. http://www.psychiatric times.com/schizophrenia/hearing-voices-and-psychiatrys-real-medical-model.

———. "Psychiatry's New Brain-Mind and the Legend of the 'Chemical Imbalance.'" *Psychiatric Times*, July 11, 2011. http://www.psychiatric times.com/blogs/ psychiatry-new-brain-mind-and-legend-chemical-imbalance.

Pies, Ronald, and Cynthia Geppert. "Clinical Depression or 'Life Sorrows'?: Distinguishing between Grief and Depression in Pastoral Care." *Ministry Magazine*, May 2015: 8-9.

Pietikäinen, Petteri. *Madness: A History*. New York: Routledge, 2015.

Porter, Roy. *Madness: A Brief History*. New York: Oxford University Press, 2002.

Ramachandran, V.S., and Sandra Blakeslee. *Phantoms in the Brain: Probing the Mysteries of the Human Mind*. New York: William Morrow and Company, 1998.

Ray, Isaac. *A Treatise on the Medical Jurisprudence of Insanity*. Boston: Charles C. Little and James Brown, 1838.

Reznek, Lawrie. *Delusions and Madness of the Masses*. New York: Rowman and Littlefield, 2010.

———. *Evil or Ill?: Justifying the Insanity Defense*. New York: Routledge, 1997.

Ruesch, Jurgen, and Gregory Bateson. *Communication: Social Matrix of Psychiatry*. New York: Norton, 1951.

Sacks, Oliver. *Hallucinations*. New York: Random House, 2012.

Satel, Sally, and Scott Lilienfeld. *Brainwashed: The Seductive Appeal of Mindless Neuroscience*. New York: Basic Books, 2013.

Scull, Andrew. *A Very Short Introduction*. New York: Oxford Press, 2011.

———. *Madness in Civilization: A Cultural History of Insanity from the Bible to Freud, from the Madhouse to Modern Medicine*. Princeton, NJ: Princeton University Press, 2015.

Shorter, Edward. *A History of Psychiatry: From the Era of the Asylum to the Age of the Prozac*. New York: John Wiley and Sons, 1997.

Soreff, Stephen M., and George McNeil. *Handbook of Psychiatric Differential Diagnosis*. Littleton, MA: PSG Publishing, 1987.

"Undermining Morals." Citizen's Commission on Human Rights UK. http://www.cchr.org.uk/psychiatric-drugs/undermining-morals/.

Van der Kolk, Bessel. *The Body Keeps the Score: Brain, Mind, and Body in the Healing of Trauma*. New York: Penguin, 2014.

Watters, Ethan, and Richard Ofshe. *Therapy's Delusions: The Myth of the Unconscious and the Exploitation of Today's Walking Worried*. New York: Simon and Schuster, 1999.

Weiss, Kenneth J., and the Group for the Advancement of Psychiatry. "A Trip Through the History of Psychiatry." *Psychiatric Times Online*, November 7, 2017. http://www.psychiatrictimes.com/blogs/history-psychiatry/trip-through-history-psychiatry?GUID=31158D64-F01A-4DEA-AC1A-D3CE843FC9BC&rememberme=1&ts=14112017.

Whitaker, Robert. *Anatomy of an Epidemic: Magic Bullets, Psychiatric Drugs, and the Astonishing Rise of Mental Illness in America*. New York: Broadway Books, 2015.

Whitfield, Charles L. *The Truth about Mental Illness: Choices for Healing*. Deerfield Beach, FL: Health Communications, 2004.

Wyhe, John van. "The History of Phrenology on the Web." http://www.historyofphrenology.org.uk/overview.htm

Yadav, Tarun, Yatan Pal Singh Balhara, and Dinesh Kumar Kataria. "Pseudocyesis Versus Delusion of Pregnancy: Differential Diagnoses to be Kept in Mind." *Indian Journal of Psychological Medicine* 34, no. 1 (Jan-Mar, 2012): 82–84.

Made in the USA
Monee, IL
13 February 2025

12129306R00118